The DBT Skills Workbook for Parents of Teens

The Ultimate Guide to Help Your Teen Manage Difficult Emotions, Increase Awareness, and Strengthen Coping Skills

Table of Contents

Introduction

As a parent, raising a teenager can be a fulfilling yet challenging experience. As your child navigates the turbulent waters of adolescence, it's natural to feel overwhelmed and unsure of how to support them effectively. The DBT Skills Workbook for Parents of Teens provides a comprehensive guide on navigating this critical phase of your child's life using Dialectical Behavior Therapy (DBT) skills. This book equips you with practical strategies and tools to strengthen your relationship with your teenager, improve communication, and help them develop essential life skills. Whether you're dealing with conflict, emotional dysregulation, school difficulties, or other problems common during this critical life stage, this workbook will show you how to harness DBT skills to create a steady and supportive foundation for your teen.

The book is organized into ten chapters covering the essential topics relating to teenage parenting. Chapters are divided into easily digestible concepts so you can find what you're looking for. You'll learn how DBT skills can fortify the bedrock of your relationship with your teen while teaching them valuable life lessons and helping them develop emotional intelligence and coping skills.

Even if you're not very involved with your child, this book is insightful and empowering. You can create a supportive environment to help your child navigate their chaotic adolescence without facing unnecessary obstacles. The DBT Skills workbook will help you guide your teenager, promoting resilience, self-confidence, and independence. You'll learn to encourage maturity, personal accountability, problem-solving, and other essential life skills. This book will challenge you to think outside the box and teach you how to stay calm, be compassionate, and figure out effective responses using your authentic strengths. By learning and practicing DBT skills, you prepare yourself to respond better to the challenges your teenager faces and equip them with the tools to navigate the complexities of adulthood.

The techniques and strategies outlined in this book are not only applicable to specific situations but also a foundation for building a solid framework for personal growth and development. With each chapter, you will gain a deeper understanding of your teenager's emotional needs and how best to provide them with the tools to develop into emotionally healthy and productive adults.

This workbook challenges you, as a parent, to look closer at yourself and your way of parenting. You will learn to identify and manage your triggers, how you think, and modes of communication. You'll determine how your history affects how you parent and be more aware of your thoughts, emotions, and tendencies. This self-reflection will empower you to better respond to the challenges of parenting a teenager and teach you to make constructive statements and express yourself skillfully, with compassion, and without judgment or criticism.

The DBT Skills Workbook for Parents of Teens is more than a book; it's your roadmap to developing a deeper understanding of yourself as a parent. It will help you find peace and calm in your relationship with your teenager and guide you as you live up to your true potential in the most important role of your life—parenting.

Chapter 1: An Introduction to DBT for Parents

DBT is psychotherapy first introduced in the late 80s by Dr. Marsha Linehan to deal with the high suicide rate among people diagnosed with borderline personality disorder (BPD). It is an integrative approach combining intensive individual therapy sessions with group skills training to teach powerful coping and communication mechanisms.

It has proven very effective for many people on the autism spectrum, in substance abuse recovery, and those diagnosed with BPD, among other mental health conditions. DBT is also used in school systems to help teens and young adults deal with emotional volatility, social pressures, and academic struggles.

DBT is an intense, demanding program focusing on teaching skills for thinking, feeling, and acting in more adaptive ways in the face of anxiety and emotional instability. It teaches "radical acceptance" of how things are, how to change what can be changed, and accept what can't be changed using combined mindfulness practice, coping skills, and behavioral changes.

Why Is DBT Necessary?

Teenagers often have difficulty dealing with the intense feelings of being an adolescent. They struggle to regulate their emotions, which is positive and healthy for themselves and those around them. They also struggle with emotional regulation because they are constantly bombarded with information from the environment, friends, family members, and other social spaces, from the internet to games to TV.

Teenagers tend to struggle with emotional regulation due to their wide range of emotions.

https://unsplash.com/photos/kFk3ji9x07k?utm_source=unsplash&utm_medium=referral&utm_content=creditShareLink

As they go deeper into their teen years, they care about more things and feel a wider range of emotions. They struggle with developing a sense of independence against the backdrop of their parent's attempts to keep them safe, guiding them through childhood. It increases overwhelmed and helplessness when dealing with their emotions and others around them.

DBT helps teens learn appropriate coping skills for themselves and even teach their friends. It teaches them to identify the urge to do a negative action, practice mindfulness of this urge, and think through actions that are more future-focused and positive instead of impulsive or negative. Eventually, these skills become automatic reactions, and these children can use their mental energy to focus on what they want to do instead of what they shouldn't.

DBT is more directly applicable to teens because most are perfectionists or self-critical when making mistakes. DBT is about accepting self and others, even when things are challenging and don't always go your way. For some teens, this can help manage their impulsivity and risk-taking patterns. It can help others connect with their family and friends better. DBT is useful for adults because it teaches people how to recognize when they are in the grip of an emotional storm and how to *get out of the storm* and move to more balanced ways of thinking, feeling, and behaving.

What Does DBT Have to Offer You and Your Teenager?

Perhaps your teen has been struggling with their emotions regarding schoolwork, personal relationships, friendships, and family. They can't get a handle on their emotions or understand why they feel the way they do. They often get into explosive arguments with family and friends, isolate themselves from others, and might even self-harm. They keep getting into trouble at school or with the authorities because they cannot deal with conflict and stress positively and healthily. Their self-esteem is at an all-time low, and they become increasingly frustrated with themselves because they feel they can never get things right, be good enough, or achieve what they want.

DBT is perfect for dealing with these issues because it teaches adolescents to immerse themselves in the present moment whenever possible instead of worrying about what has happened in the past or what could happen in the future. They learn to deal with the current situation as is, not as they wish it would be. It helps them learn to let go of what they cannot change, which relieves them of a lot of pressure.

It is natural to be concerned about your child. You want them to feel better, safer, and more capable so they can be happy at school and home. You want to know that they won't be taken advantage of by other teens who are more socially savvy or manipulative. You want them to be successful and feel good about themselves, which makes you feel good about yourself. You want them to appreciate the positive aspects of their lives so they can see the bigger picture and enjoy themselves more.

DBT can help you achieve all these goals. It teaches your teen how to have a better relationship with their feelings and deal with the highs and lows of adolescence. They will learn to identify "hot moments" when emotions are high, and many negative thoughts swirl around in their minds. It teaches them strategies for pulling themselves out of an emotional funk when they cannot see a way out. It also teaches them how to avoid getting into that emotional state in the first place. When not in an emotional funk, they often have a lot of energy they don't know what to do with. Having access to skills for changing their feelings, thoughts, and behaviors when anxiety is high can give them back the motivation, energy, and enthusiasm that is so hard to come by when depressed and discouraged.

DBT offers skills for dealing with emotions and behaviors provoking negative reactions in others. It allows your child to approach frightening or uncomfortable situations without fear or embarrassment. It brings newfound confidence to the table and helps them feel safer in the world.

Lastly, DBT allows adolescents to develop a stronger ability to take constructive action toward goals instead of relying on negative emotions or actions to get what they want. It teaches them to leverage their strengths and cultivate healthy habits that give them a clearer head and a more positive outlook.

How Does It Work?

DBT is an integrative approach using combined skills training in regulated breathing, mindfulness of thoughts and feelings, distress tolerance, emotion regulation, impulse control, and interpersonal effectiveness. It teaches teenagers to identify their triggers for negative actions, practice these in a safe environment, and replace those negative actions with healthier behaviors.

The skills are taught over a series of sessions. During the initial sessions, your child will learn to identify negative emotions, what triggered them, and how their brains process them. They will learn to regulate their breathing, which helps them make sense of the emotions they are experiencing and how they are processing them through their bodies. They learn about triggers, how to identify them, and what they can do to avoid getting into a negative emotional spiral. It helps them stay in the here and now instead of getting lost in their thoughts about the past or future. Moreover, they learn to be more mindful of their thoughts, neutralizing the emotional strength of the negative ones and replacing them with neutral or positive ones. Lastly, DBT teaches them to practice coping strategies when those emotions are too strong to manage.

Core Modules of DBT

Four core modules are taught in the DBT course:

1. Mindfulness
2. Distress tolerance
3 Emotion regulation
4. Interpersonal effectiveness.

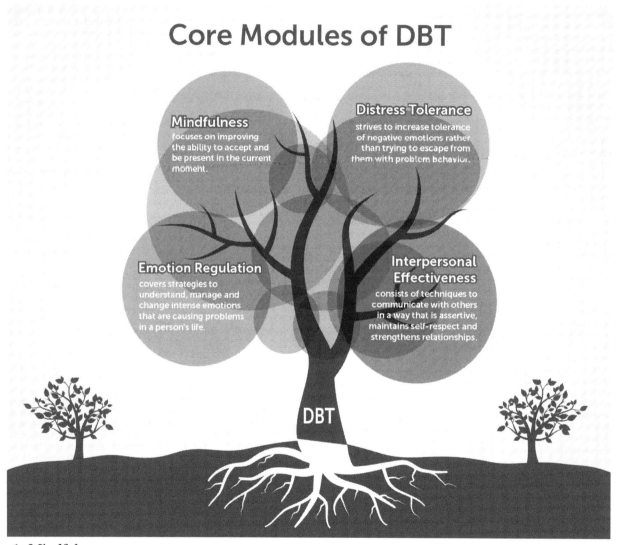

Core Modules of DBT

Mindfulness
focuses on improving the ability to accept and be present in the current moment.

Distress Tolerance
strives to increase tolerance of negative emotions rather than trying to escape from them with problem behavior.

Emotion Regulation
covers strategies to understand, manage and change intense emotions that are causing problems in a person's life.

Interpersonal Effectiveness
consists of techniques to communicate with others in a way that is assertive, maintains self-respect and strengthens relationships.

DBT

1. Mindfulness

Mindfulness is the first core skill taught in DBT. It teaches teenagers a method for observing and experiencing their present moment without judgment. Often, adolescents get caught up in their thoughts and emotions, believing they are a reality or experienced by everyone else, too. Mindfulness teaches them to see thoughts and emotions are just that: thoughts and emotions. They come, stay for a while, and then go away.

2. Distress Tolerance

Distress tolerance is the second core skill taught in DBT. It teaches teenagers how to gain freedom from overwhelmed and emotionally unstable effects. Distress tolerance teaches them how to be compassionate with themselves when they struggle. It builds emotional strength so they can move through negative emotions more quickly and decisively, teaching them to become more comfortable with uncomfortable feelings.

3. Emotion Regulation

Emotion regulation is the third core skill taught in DBT. Emotion regulation aims to help teens identify and accurately label their emotions. Emotional awareness enhances coping with emotions and prevents severe emotional episodes from happening when waves of negative feelings are present. It teaches them to be curious about and ask themselves questions about their emotions so they can control their thoughts.

4. Interpersonal Effectiveness

Interpersonal effectiveness is the fourth and final core skill taught in DBT. Interpersonal effectiveness teaches adolescents to talk to people about their thoughts and feelings, listen to them, and meet their needs. It teaches them to see many different ways they can approach situations, which is a difficult skill for some adolescents to acquire on their own. Interpersonal effectiveness offers a structure to help them build healthy and functional relationships with others.

How Can These Modules Help?

Mindfulness is the ability to be in the moment and live in the present. Teenagers who are not mindful can get caught up in their thoughts and emotions. It leads them to focus only on themselves and their negative feelings, preventing them from living a balanced life. Also, when they are not mindful of their present state, they might act or speak emotionally without thinking about other people's needs or how these actions might affect others.

Distress tolerance is recognizing and working through distress. One of the hallmarks of adolescence is that teens feel overwhelmed, upset, and desperate in their constant search for friends, popularity, and acceptance; this is normal. But it's a time to grow up, form new friendships, and step outside their comfort zone. But sometimes, it can feel too much to handle. DBT teaches teenagers how to deal with these emotions, channeling the energy and returning to a place of reflection instead of getting lost in them. Distress tolerance teaches teenagers that instead of feeling stuck in their feelings, they can learn to be more compassionate with themselves when struggling and give themselves the space to feel better. Adolescents should develop the skills to recognize and work through their distress. Unfortunately, many teens are not taught how to cope with distress constructively. They are expected to figure it out independently and suffer the consequences. However, there is another better way, and you can help.

Emotion regulation is the ability to be aware of and understand your emotions. Often, adolescents feel overwhelmed or afraid of certain emotions because they are experiencing them for the first time. They might not understand what feeling jealous means or what triggers anger, leading them to acknowledge only their negative feelings and thoughts instead of all the emotions, positive ones included. With DBT, teenagers are taught to acknowledge all their positive and negative emotions without judgment. They learn to identify each emotion and use it as a tool for better thinking and problem-solving. Emotion regulation teaches them how to reach a point where they are comfortable and confident with their emotions.

Interpersonal effectiveness is communicating with people about your thoughts and feelings. Adolescents are not taught how to talk about their thoughts and feelings with each other, leading them to feel frustrated and shut down. Interpersonal effectiveness teaches adolescents how to talk about their thoughts, fears, opinions, and goals with others and how these are connected. These skills help develop healthy relationships, friendships, and social connections throughout life.

DBT is a goal-oriented therapy that emphasizes helping adolescents develop a more positive outlook on life. They are taught to identify their goals and to pursue them actively instead of passively, letting life happen. The idea behind this is that teens learn to set clear, realistic goals for themselves and pursue them effectively. They will feel better about themselves and be less likely to engage in self-destructive behavior.

DBT is also a family-oriented therapy. It is an excellent way for parents and other caregivers to help their teens. The family sessions provide an opportunity to learn more about your teens' emotional and behavioral patterns so you can help address potential problems before they start. Communication is an essential part of relationships, and when your teen feels comfortable talking to you about themselves and their emotions, they become more open and are more likely to come to you if they have a problem.

DBT is a family-oriented therapy.
https://www.pexels.com/photo/happy-friends-embracing-in-summer-yard-5638577/

DBT acknowledges that behavioral patterns develop in relationships over time until people eventually fall into certain roles. This therapy will help you and your child identify which of your roles are helpful and unhelpful in the family system and the behavior patterns contributing to these roles. It teaches you how to act differently from these roles to create healthier relationships and better-functioning families. By understanding the dynamics within your family system, DBT can provide you with tools and strategies to break free from harmful patterns and cultivate a more harmonious environment. Through this therapy, you and your child will gain insight into the underlying emotions and triggers that fuel these roles, allowing you to make conscious choices promoting positive change.

Together, you will explore effective communication techniques, problem-solving skills, and coping mechanisms to navigate challenges and build resilience as a family unit. Together, you will learn to communicate openly and honestly, listen without judgment, and love unconditionally. By learning to be truly present in your life and your child's, you will conquer the challenges of adolescence and set the stage for a lifetime of healthy, happy relationships.

Key Takeaways

- The DBT approach acknowledges the link between emotions, thoughts, actions, and mood. It is designed to teach teenagers how to identify their emotional triggers and develop coping strategies.

- Adolescence can be challenging, and teenagers must learn how to manage discomfort constructively. Unfortunately, most teenagers are not taught how to do so. The distress tolerance program in DBT helps teenagers become more self-aware and develop communication and mindfulness skills, enabling them to cope successfully with their emotions and discover their true selves.

- Interpersonal effectiveness is another aspect of DBT that equips teenagers with the skills to express their thoughts, fears, views, and aspirations to others healthily. These skills enable them to build healthier relationships, friendships, and social connections throughout their lives.

- DBT is a family-based therapy that addresses the challenges of family life and the development of healthy interpersonal relationships.

- DBT's goal-oriented approach helps teenagers develop a positive outlook on life. They are encouraged to define their goals and actively work towards achieving them rather than passively letting life happen to them.

- As a parent, you can get involved in your teenager's DBT treatment to become part of the therapeutic process.

- DBT recognizes that behavioral patterns emerge in relationships over time, leading people to fall into certain roles. This therapy helps you and your teenager identify which roles are helpful and unhelpful in the family system and the behaviors contributing to these roles.

- In sum, DBT teaches you and your teenager how to be present in your lives, setting the stage for a lifetime of healthy and happy relationships.

Chapter 2: Navigating the Teenage Emotional Rollercoaster

It doesn't matter if your child is a typically cheerful and outgoing or moody teenager who gets mad at the slightest thing. As parents, you'll likely experience both extremes as your teen grows up. It's easy to blame your teen's moodiness on hormones, but there's a lot more to it than that. After all, emotions such as anger, frustration, and irritability aren't limited to adolescence. They can appear in children of any age, but adolescence brings them to the forefront.

A teen's emotions can change quickly.
https://www.pexels.com/photo/shallow-focus-photo-of-girl-smiling-260.5637/

Sometimes, your teen is so happy they can hardly contain themselves. They might walk around with a big smile on their face, often forgiving everyone for the most trivial things. This ever-present happiness will likely come without much reason and is not forced; your teen feels good about life, and everything seems to go their way. During these moments, you might catch yourself reminiscing about the carefree days of your youth when joy seemed to flow effortlessly. But as quickly as the happiness comes, it can also vanish, leaving your teen feeling sad or melancholy in a way that isn't easy to understand. Remember, these mood swings are a natural part of adolescence as your teen navigates the complexities of their changing emotions and identity.

During this stage, they experience a multitude of physical, hormonal, and psychological changes, often like major shifts in personality. As they strive to establish their unique identity, they could encounter moments of self-doubt and confusion. It's your job to offer support and understanding during these times, even if it is challenging with a child who repeatedly tells you they don't need your help. Remember, like unpredictable weather, their moods can shift rapidly, leaving them feeling lost in a sea of uncertainty.

Not everyone is affected by these emotions similarly, especially at such a young age. Different people are affected by different things, often for very different reasons. For example, some teenagers might love school and are on their way to near-perfect grades. Others might hate school and couldn't care less about getting good grades. One teenager might handle peer pressure well, but another is easily swayed by their mates' reactions. The bottom line is that no matter how similar teens seem, they are still individuals who respond very differently to various stimuli.

As a parent, you play a pivotal role in helping your child navigate these sometimes volatile emotions. It might very well take you to the brink of sanity, but it's also a valuable learning experience for you both as they grow and move away from their family's protective and nurturing embrace. Your teen is likely already showing signs of wanting to become more independent and will most certainly be asserting their preferences and opinions more often. You must respect their individuality and independence, even if you don't always agree with them. They are exploring their identities and establishing their place in the world. It can lead to conflicts and disagreements between parents and teens as you both navigate this new territory. But the truth is, as they become more independent, their world expands, offering them opportunities for important and valuable social connections. Also, it means an increase in personal space, which can make it difficult for you to understand them when they aren't telling you what they need or want directly.

Feeling shut out or left in the dark as a parent is frustrating and even hurtful. However, remember, this is a normal part of their development, not a reflection of your relationship. Instead of taking it personally, focus on maintaining open lines of communication and creating a safe and non-judgmental space where they feel comfortable expressing themselves. By actively listening and showing genuine interest in their lives, they will feel more motivated to open up to you. When they're ready to talk, a warm smile or a simple nod of encouragement can make all the difference.

Understanding the Rollercoaster

As teenagers go through their teenage years, they experience a range of emotions that go beyond mere mood swings. They undergo significant developmental events as they gain a deeper understanding of themselves and their surroundings, forge new relationships, and learn to cope with the responsibilities of young adulthood. These experiences are essential for every teenager, regardless of personality or self-motivation.

However, the stress of these experiences can trigger intense feelings that are challenging to comprehend. These emotions are amplified by the circumstances of teenage life, such as changing relationships with friends, parents, and other authority figures. Teenagers may feel aimless and dissatisfied with their lives, and this emptiness may seem out of place and inexplicable. Alternatively, these feelings could be linked to a meaningful or traumatic event that occurred during a vulnerable time.

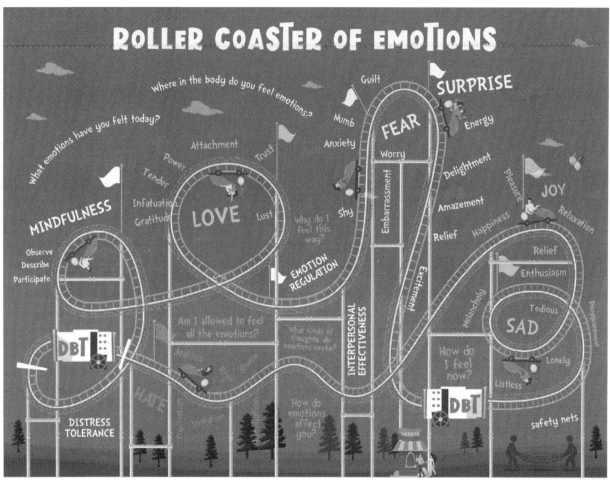

Teenagers are also affected by hormonal changes that lead to heightened arousal. Their brains, bodies, and emotional regulation abilities are still developing. Sometimes, these changes can cause inner turmoil that cannot be contained, resulting in emotional outbursts at home or school. Thankfully, these emotional outbursts often dissipate once the brain has caught up with the rest of the body. Psychologists have identified four core factors that are significantly influential in the emotional volatility of your teenager:

1. Hormonal Changes
2. Brain development
3. Social pressures
4. The quest for identity

Hormonal Changes

Teenagers undergo hormonal changes that often trigger jealousy, stress, and insecurity. Excessive levels of the stress hormone cortisol can trigger anxiety in teens who are not used to feeling so much pressure. Adrenaline is another hormone commonly referred to as fight or flight, which creates a sense of extreme urgency and sensitivity to threats in a teen's environment.

Research has shown that teens who experience high stress or low trust levels in the social environment can experience more emotional volatility. However, these emotions are rarely tied to one specific event. They are as unpredictable as rain and often emerge when teens least expect it. Emotional outbursts triggered by hormonal changes such as puberty can last for days, weeks, or even months, but they will eventually subside. Distress tolerance, or the ability to recognize and handle a painful feeling or emotion constructively, is an important skill that develops over time but can be encouraged during adolescence. Typically, teens exhibiting high distress tolerance can move through their emotions and face them head-on; this is called resilience. However, teens experiencing low distress tolerance might not be prepared for the intensity of their feelings and lack the coping skills necessary to solve their problems. These feelings can often lead to upsetting thoughts that spiral out of control.

Brain Development

The brain is a complex organ undergoing constant changes throughout a person's lifetime. This process, known as neuroplasticity, allows the development of new neural pathways that aren't always affected by age or genetics. This process is triggered by things seen, felt, and experienced in a person's life, which alters the neural pathways transmitting information throughout the brain.

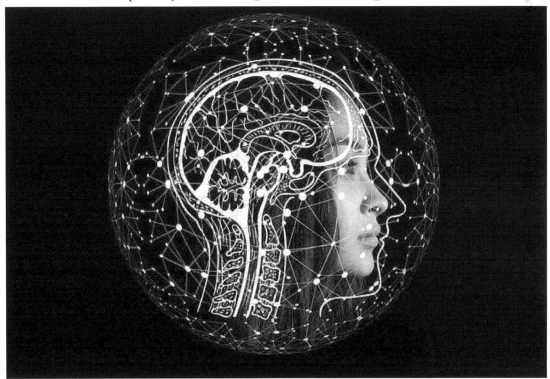

The teenage years involve dramatic physical changes that impact the brain's development.
https://pixabay.com/illustrations/artificial-intelligence-brain-4389372/

The teenage years are marked by dramatic physical changes impacting the brain's development. Your teenager's brain is growing and changing at an exponential rate. It is also peaking in metabolic activity, learning, and information processing. Like hormonal changes, the brain development of a teenager is unpredictable. The cortex, particularly the prefrontal cortex, controls executive functions, such as planning, organization, and attention span. This area of the brain doesn't stop growing until a person's early 20s in most people. This immaturity in the brain often corresponds to immaturity in behavior and decision-making. Teens can be impulsive due to their lack of impulse control and struggle to think through situations before taking action, often acting on instinct or emotions rather than considering the potential consequences. This impulsivity is exacerbated by the sensations of novelty and risk linked to their exposure to new social, academic, and physical environments.

Teenagers are also affected by the mesocortical dopamine system, which regulates motivation and pleasure. This dopamine system is responsible for the wanting, craving, and seeking rewards that drive your teenager's behavior. Hence, teens are more obsessed with seeking new rewards in their environment, such as sex, drugs, and alcohol. It's also why they are more risk-seeking than adults due to their lower paranoia and anxiety levels. Furthermore, teenagers have difficulty regulating their emotions, experiencing intense mood swings that can seem erratic to those around them. These emotional ups and downs can further contribute to their unpredictable nature, as their reactions to different situations can vary greatly from one moment to the next. Mindfulness and awareness can help your teen cope with these manifestations of adolescent behavior. By practicing mindfulness, teenagers can better understand and accept their emotions and reactions. This heightened self-awareness allows them to pause and reflect before impulsively responding to a situation, leading to more thoughtful and intentional actions.

Social Pressures

A common element of emotional volatility is the effect peer pressure can have on a teenager. Typically, teenagers are highly attuned to what's happening in their social environment; this influences their decision-making processes. For example, they might try to fit in with the crowd and adopt behaviors that seem appropriate for their social environment. Teenagers might also change their beliefs if the crowd changes their perceptions of what is valuable or funny. In extreme cases, this can lead to groupthink, where a teenager loses touch with their values as they conform to the standards of their peer group.

Teens are highly sensitive to the expectations of authority figures, particularly teachers and parents, who have higher social status. It can make them highly reliant on the opinions of those around them, which could shape how they perceive themselves and their place in society. Teenagers struggling with emotional instability often seek people or activities supporting their unstable moods and emotions. They might gravitate toward friends who validate their feelings or engage in activities that slow down the rollercoaster and distract them from their emotions. This search for validation and support can sometimes lead them down unpleasant paths, like substance abuse or engaging in risky behaviors.

On the other hand, it can also drive them to seek healthier outlets, like joining support groups or participating in creative activities to help them constructively express their emotions. The influence of peers and authority figures on a teenager's emotional well-being is undeniable. Understanding this dynamic will help you proactively approach your teenager's emotional stability.

The Quest for Identity

A major theme emerging throughout adolescence is the quest for identity. During adolescence, your teenager strives to create an identity they can call their own. It involves clarifying and challenging existing perceptions of themselves and ideals about others in their environment. For example, they might define their sense of self in traditional gender roles, which places them in one of two categories: male or female. If they identify as female, they will attempt to internalize femininity by dressing and behaving in a way that confirms this identity. They would also seek others to validate this identity, like friends, family, and future partners. At the same time, they could challenge traditional gender roles by rejecting rigid gender stereotypes and trying to express themselves to conform to their perceived sense of self.

A common theme throughout the quest for identity is the relationship between your teenager and their mates. Your teenager is likely to feel peer pressure to conform to specific ideals and expectations. These can range from dressing a certain way or emulating the behaviors of popular celebrities to experimenting with alcohol, drugs, and sex. It can lead them down a path of self-doubt, disrupting their sense of identity and making them delusional about who they truly are. They can become obsessed with trying to fit in, ultimately leading to shyness and insecurity.

As your teenager begins to define a sense of self, they are also developing their unique values. This step is important in their personal identity. Yet, it can be difficult for them to articulate these values because they might not be in touch with their own morality. Moral values differ from the sense of right and wrong taught by adults. Their moral values are more closely aligned with their internal sense of right and wrong, based on emotions, intuition, and personal experiences. It is an important distinction because it helps you understand why teenagers can make uncharacteristic decisions seemingly against their best interests. You can help them clarify their values by getting them to describe what they believe in. It might sound complex, but it's quite straightforward, as getting teenagers to articulate their beliefs is more about listening than anything else.

Being a teenager's parent is an exciting time but can also be an exhausting and demanding experience. You are fostering this extraordinary process of self-discovery that is only available to them at this age. Teenagers can change dramatically at any moment, which can pose a serious challenge to their parents. Fortunately, there is much you can do to support your teenager's emotional stability. Keeping track of their emotional trajectory will help you build a relationship based on trust and understanding instead of fear and suspicion. You can discuss changes in their behavior or moods openly and honestly so that you can learn from each other's experiences. In time, your teenager will trust you, making it even easier to be honest with them about their changing emotions and behaviors. A positive cycle of communication will emerge, giving you greater control as you guide your teenager through this exciting and challenging process of human development.

Chapter 3: Mindfulness for Teens and Parents

Mindfulness is a buzzword that's a lot harder to define than it sounds. Usually, mindfulness describes two things: the practice of meditation and the ability to pay attention to current moment-to-moment experiences. Essentially, it means being nonjudgmental and open-minded during an activity or situation. In parenting, mindfulness focuses on the present and understanding your role. For teens, it is looking inside yourself to see what is happening internally.

How Mindfulness Can Help You and Your Teen

Parents and their teenagers don't always connect as they could or should because teen minds are constantly in motion, and their emotions are flying high. It's hard to have meaningful conversations when their thoughts are scattered, thanks to distractions like social media, video games, and homework.

Furthermore, teens' emotions can get in the way of communication. They might be embarrassed by something that happened at school or a friend's house and hold it in until it explodes unexpectedly. It creates an "us versus them" mentality between parents and their children—that they are separate people instead of one unit. Mindfulness allows parents to learn more about their children and allows teens to understand themselves and their emotions. They can also bond with their parents and actively learn from them.

Mindfulness allows teens and parents to bond.

Our culture places enormous pressure on teens to succeed and be the best—from winning the spelling bee at the local library to getting accepted into their dream Ivy League school. It's hard to feel accepted when you fall short of other people's expectations or when you feel you've disappointed your parents. Moreover, teens are desperate to fit in. They want to be like their favorite celebrities, wear the right shoes, and make friends. From the outside looking in, it might appear they have it all together, but they don't. They feel fear and anxiety just as adults do, and social media pressures do not help them feel better about themselves.

Mindfulness can help your teen gain a better perspective on themselves, which is the key to feeling more fulfilled and less anxious. They will feel more connected to you because they can communicate more openly and honestly. Mindfulness allows teens to develop a deeper understanding of their thoughts and emotions, which helps them navigate the pressures and expectations of social media. By practicing mindfulness, teenagers can learn to recognize negative self-talk and replace it with positive affirmations, boosting their self-esteem and confidence. This newfound self-awareness and self-acceptance can bridge the gap between teens and their parents, fostering a stronger bond built on trust and open communication.

Make Mindfulness Fun

Many barriers between parents and their teens are emotional, not physical, meaning they don't have a physical workaround. A mindful parent is an empathetic parent, and it can mean a lot to a teenager who feels embarrassed, humiliated, anxious, or frustrated. As a parent, you can set an example of how to relax, breathe, and let go of emotions when they get in the way of enjoying life. It won't work for everyone, but for those open-minded to its practice and willing to try something different, this might be one of the most important things you could do for your teen.

You might have heard the term "attachment parenting," which focuses on connecting with babies and children early in life through touch, words, and play. Mindfulness is a natural extension of attachment parenting because it teaches compassion, empathy, and kindness—something most people could use a little more of these days.

Meditating with your child early on is an extension of attachment parenting.
https://www.pexels.com/photo/adorable-african-american-kid-with-young-mom-practicing-yoga-in-lotus-pose-7353064/

For a parent, learning and practicing mindfulness will help you read your teen's behavioral cues better. You will recognize what they need most by helping them become more aware of their thoughts and emotions. It allows you to respond to changes in their behavior in ways they will appreciate. Ultimately, it's about acceptance. Mindfulness teaches everyone to live in the moment, which helps you understand your role rather than trying to change it. If you can accept yourself and their situation, you can tackle problems or challenges without losing your cool.

Mindfulness Exercises for Teens and Parents

If you want to help your child start mindfulness, try these exercises:

1. Box Breathing Exercise: Mindfulness starts with the breath. Taking a few deep breaths can slow your racing thoughts and turn your attention inward. You can do this with your child or teach them to do it on their own. To begin:

- **Step one:** Sit comfortably and close your eyes.

- **Step two:** Begin by observing your breath. Notice the air entering and leaving your nose.

- **Step three:** Breathe in slowly and intentionally. Feel the air coming into your nostrils. As you breathe in, feel your chest expand. This inhale should last four seconds.

- **Step four:** Hold your breath for three seconds and then exhale slowly, smoothly, and gently. This exhale should last for four seconds. As you breathe out, feel your chest contract.

- **Step five:** Observe each breath and calm the mind with each inhale and exhale.

- **Step six:** Continue this for at least two minutes. This is a great exercise to do anytime, anywhere, because you don't need any special equipment, and it can calm you down when you're upset.

2. Meditation: When you start a mindfulness practice, you must begin with meditation basics: sitting or lying still with your eyes closed, focusing on your breathing, and tuning out distractions. Start with five minutes a day and build from there. It's better to do this for too short a time than for too long initially, which can make your child antsy or irritated. A good meditation that is beginner-friendly is the "body scan." To begin:

- **Step one:** Start by standing (or sitting if you prefer).

- **Step two:** Next, take a deep inhale and exhale slowly.

- **Step three:** Now, you want to feel your whole body. Imagine an invisible energy working its way through each limb, starting with your fingers or toes.

- **Step four:** Breathe and feel. Focus on the energy as it takes you through your hands and wrists, up your arms, through your shoulders, upper back, neck, down the spine, and out the bottom of your feet.

- **Step five:** Repeat this feeling process again, this time going in the opposite direction, starting with your toes and working up. Do this one or two more times.

- **Step six:** Finally, let your body relax, imagining all that energy reducing in intensity and flowing out of you. Know that the energy is around you, but don't focus on it. Instead, just breathe in, relax, and breathe out.

3. Awareness: Creating an intended mind map about how different events or situations make you feel can help give you more insight into your emotions and behavior. It is a great exercise for teens because it teaches them to accept their emotions rather than trying to change them. It's also an effective way to compile the lessons you've learned from your experiences. To begin:

- **Step one:** Think about an event that made you feel a certain way that you aren't proud of. For example, maybe you were rude to someone yesterday or lost your temper this morning, and now you regret it.

- **Step two:** Write down how that event made you feel and why.

- **Step three:** Now put a plus sign next to the feelings you want to keep or grow into and a negative sign next to the ones you want to change.

- **Step four:** Repeat these steps for other events that made you feel a certain way.

- **Step five:** When you're done, review your experience and see what you can learn from it. Emotions can be scary, but they are not beyond our control. Learn to accept them, and use this exercise to improve your reaction to them in the future.

4. Mindful Communication: Mindful communication is sharing your feelings, thoughts, and ideas compassionately and non-judgmentally without becoming defensive or forceful. It is the oil that helps your relationship run smoothly and last for years. A good exercise to help with this is the "I" statement. To begin:

- **Step one:** Start a conversation with your child. Tell them you want to talk with them about something important.

- **Step two:** Next, use "I statements. For example, let's say your daughter is upset and hasn't spoken to you all day. You can say, "I feel sad when you refuse to talk to me."

- **Step three:** Next, your child should respond with "I" statements as well. For example, "I felt..." "I didn't..." "I think..."

- **Step four:** Continue with "I" statements until both of you feel that you're on the same page about what happened.

Potential Obstacles of Mindfulness with Teens

It's better to be realistic about the benefits of mindfulness and the challenges involved. Here are some aspects you could have trouble with during your journey:

1. **It Takes Time:** While practicing mindfulness is beneficial in the long run, it can take a while to see results. Some people notice changes within a week or two, while others need to work on it daily for months before seeing improvements. Give yourself and your child's mind time to adjust to this new way of thinking and behaving—it can save everyone a lot of stress, fighting, and heartache in the end.

Mindfulness takes time, making it a potential obstacle.
https://www.pexels.com/photo/a-clock-hanging-on-a-wall-8542504/

2. **It's Hard to Concentrate:** Regular mindfulness practice can help improve concentration. It can be troublesome for teens with attention problems. They can become frustrated when a simple exercise like focusing on their breathing becomes difficult, but this is a normal part of the learning process. Take it slow, and they will improve over time.

3. **It's Boring:** Mindfulness isn't always the most interesting activity in the world, but if you make it fun for your child, they will be more motivated to work with you and practice the awareness of their emotions and surroundings. Be creative and positive, and use games or activities that appeal to your teen's interests.

4. **Not Everyone Is Ready for Mindfulness:** While mindfulness is a great idea, it's not always the best choice for everyone. Some teens opt out of practicing mindfulness altogether because they don't agree with the process or it does not interest them. Don't force your approach on them if they aren't ready. Instead, try again in a few months when they might be more open to the idea. Appreciating your teen's opinion is the first step toward improving communication and understanding each other's needs, wants, and beliefs.

5. **You Might Have to Step Outside of Your Comfort Zone:** If you are not used to practicing mindfulness, it will take some effort, and you might have a few doubts or concerns about the process. Approach it with an open mind and be aware of your feelings, thoughts, and intentions. Remember, no one is judging you; this isn't a contest. It takes a lot of concentration, practice, and discipline, but the results are worth it.

Teens and mindfulness don't seem like they should go together, but learning to be mindful can help them relieve stress, improve their self-confidence, and foster a deeper understanding of the world around them. More importantly, it presents an exciting time to connect with your child profoundly and see their potential emerge as you become more mindful of each other. Take the first step to develop a more mindful relationship, guide them into a new world of peace, joy, patience, acceptance, and love, and let them discover how easy life becomes when they practice mindfulness.

Chapter 4: Building Resilience

Resilience is the ability to bounce back from setbacks, adapt to change, and thrive in the face of adversity. It is considered one of the most important life skills people must learn to successfully navigate life's challenges and uncertainties. Developing resilience is particularly crucial for teenagers as they face various physical, emotional, and social changes during this transformative stage of their lives. Adolescence is a time of immense growth and self-discovery but can also be filled with stress, pressure, and difficult experiences. With the increasing rates of drug abuse, domestic violence, and school shootings in society, this skill is becoming more important than ever. So, what does resilience entail? What are the necessary ingredients to build and cultivate it as a skill in teenagers? What are effective techniques for building resilience in this world?

Resilience is the ability to bounce back, like a ball, from setbacks and adapt to change.

Many theories explain how resilience develops in individuals, and most were created with adults in mind, not teenagers. Therefore, educators and therapists have spent much time trying to understand the processes of adolescent development and how they differ from an adult's experience. Since this niche of research has yet to consider how teenagers' emotions and behavior vary from adults, theories continue to develop from studies in adult groups. Some distinctions are noteworthy. For example, teenagers are more impulsive and emotionally reactive. They have a higher heart rate and a greater need for excitement. They can be completely unaware of their emotions, only to be driven by them. This heightened emotional reactivity often leads to impulsive decision-making and risky behaviors, as teenagers are more likely to prioritize immediate gratification over long-term consequences.

Resilience researchers have not yet determined how these differences contribute to developing and maintaining resilience in adolescents. With no understanding of how to handle adolescent behaviors, it is often difficult to help teenagers learn to be more resilient in a real-world situation. If we start with research from adults, it will be like trying to repair a car with a flashlight and duct tape. Acknowledging adolescent differences might make it easier to develop tools to help adolescents become more resilient. It can begin by exploring what it means to be resilient among teenagers and how they differ from adults. From there, this understanding can create new techniques for teens to build resilience.

Resilience in Teenagers

Adolescents are characterized by increased activity and emotional reactivity levels, often associated with the teen years. It likely affects how teenagers develop resilience because their emotions are closely tied to their environment. For example, if teenagers feel too much pressure to have good grades and receive a high SAT score, they could feel every failure as completely devastating. For teenagers, emotional reactions are amplified, and if they can't bounce back from the occasional failure, resilience will be harder to build.

In contrast, adults have learned to understand the importance of taking emotional risks and managing their emotions with more detachment. This ability to regulate emotions and maintain perspective is crucial for adults to navigate life's complexities. Unlike teenagers, adults have often experienced a multitude of setbacks and disappointments that shaped their understanding of failure and the necessity of resilience. They have learned that failure is not the end but rather an opportunity for growth and self-improvement. This mindset allows adults to bounce back from failures more easily as they have developed coping mechanisms and a broader perspective on what truly matters in life.

According to the American Psychological Association, four components comprise resilience: self-belief, control of emotions and thoughts, connectedness, and perception of meaning.

- **Self-belief** is the belief that a person can handle difficult situations and come out better than before. It can be strengthened by recalling when you stood up to challenges and succeeded. It helps people identify their strengths and plan to use them in the future.

- **Control of emotions and thoughts** is controlling how people think and feel instead of letting them control them. The goal is to shift from being a victim to being the master of your emotions. For example, instead of feeling sad because a friend is moving away, think and feel excited that a new vacation spot will be opening up for you both.

- **Connectedness** is building positive relationships with others and having a clear identity. Good connections with others make it easier to bounce back from difficulties because others can help when things go wrong.

- **Perception of meaning** is the degree to which a person feels they are making sense of the current situation and their role in it. Generally, people with high resiliency have a better ability to view their situation objectively; this allows them to be more adaptable to changing conditions.

Is My Child Resilient?

A number of key behaviors indicate teenagers' resilience in the face of difficulty. One example is optimism, the belief that good things will happen and bad things will disappear. Another is valuing the present more than the future, indicating that a teenager can be less worried about what might happen in the future and more focused on right now. Another important trait is their ability to make adaptive choices or choices right for their circumstances instead of being swayed by fads and trends. Adaptive choices are being good at taking advantage of opportunities and realizing when a situation calls for adjustment. So, is your teen optimistic, valuing the present, and adapting to situations? These are some ways you can tell if your teen is resilient.

Factors Contributing to Resilience in Teenagers

Researchers have identified some significant contributing factors that make teenagers more or less resilient. You can control these actions or factors to increase your teenager's chance to be resilient when needed.

- **Supportive Relationships**

Supportive relationships are relationships with a positive impact on how a teenager reacts. These relationships will likely make teenagers feel more confident about getting through hard times and help them find strength when they fall.

- **Clear Identity**

Teens with a clear identity tend to be more resilient.
https://pixabay.com/vectors/id-laminated-passport-document-1605162/

A clear identity increases your teen's chances of resilience because it gives them more ability to focus on problems and turn them into opportunities instead of being weighed down by their self-image.

- **Engaging in Positive Activities**

Engaging in positive activities like sports or hobbies will help your teenager feel a sense of accomplishment, allowing them to see human-on-human interactions and practice a variety of social skills.

- **Problem-Solving Skills**

Many teenagers are natural problem solvers, but the more your teen learns about problem-solving, the better they will be at finding effective solutions.

- **Understanding of Psychological Principles**

This cognitive ability allows a teenager to understand the reasons behind their emotions and actions. Mastering their emotions makes using these emotions constructively easier, rather than using them against themselves or others.

- **A Positive Mindset**

Teens with a positive mindset can see even the most negative situations as opportunities for learning, growing, and self-discovery. They develop confidence, motivating them to find solutions instead of getting upset by what's happening.

- **Flexibility**

As the saying goes, it's better to be flexible than right. A flexible mindset makes adapting to their ever-changing world easier for your teen.

DBT-Based Strategies for Building Resilience

There are multiple ways to help teenagers build resilience, but DBT-based strategies can be used in almost any situation. These strategies focus on building teenagers' self-confidence and increasing their ability to tolerate difficult emotions like sadness, fear, and anger.

- **Mindfulness**

Mindfulness practices like a mantra, mindful walking, and paced breathing can help a teenager calm their mind and respond instead of reacting when faced with difficult emotions. Any exercise requiring observing thoughts, feelings, and sensory experiences without being caught up in them will help your teenager develop an awareness of their bodily experiences and distinguish between what is and isn't real. This awareness can be particularly helpful for teenagers experiencing heightened emotions and struggling to differentiate between their thoughts and reality. Practicing mindfulness, they learn to recognize and acknowledge their emotions without becoming overwhelmed. It can provide a sense of control and empowerment as they realize they can choose how to respond to challenging situations rather than react impulsively.

- **Reframing**

Reframing is a skill associated with emotional regulation, which is the ability to change how people perceive stressful situations. For example, instead of feeling helpless about a problem because it's overwhelming and not going well, teens can learn to see it as an opportunity for learning and growth. This skill can be mastered by looking at the same problem from different angles and identifying the elements of the problem. For example, if teenagers face social rejection, they can look at what they did wrong, what their friend did wrong, or the situation before it turned sour. By eliminating the blame and learning to see things as right and wrong instead of good or bad, teenagers learn to feel better about themselves and their place in the world.

Moreover, adopting a multi-dimensional perspective helps teenagers to develop open-mindedness and flexibility in their thinking. It allows them to recognize that multiple factors often influence a situation, and there might not always be a straightforward or black-and-white solution. This understanding promotes a more nuanced and compassionate approach toward problem-solving, encouraging teenagers to consider different perspectives and the diverse needs and experiences of those involved. By broadening their worldview and embracing complexity, teenagers become more effective communicators and collaborators, fostering healthier relationships and contributing positively to their communities.

- Self-Control

Controlling impulses and emotions is a vital skill for teens. One way to build self-control is learning to pause, breathe, and consider the consequences of an action rather than reacting automatically. Self-control helps teenagers avoid many conflicting situations. For example, let's say they're angry about someone else's behavior. In that case, they can learn to take a break before saying what's on their mind instead of blurting out something hurtful or making an impulsive decision that might have long-term consequences.

- Self-Soothing

Many people don't realize that self-soothing is a critical skill for building resilience because it allows people to handle stress better and calm themselves when upset. Self-soothing can be as simple as taking a few deep breaths, saying something nice to yourself, or doing something active or engaging. For example, if you notice your child is upset after a conflict, you can help them learn self-soothing methods, like taking a walk, talking to a friend, or practicing a hobby like drawing or baking, depending on your child's interests.

The Role of Parents in Promoting Resilience

Your teen will need your support to build resilience. One way to support them is by helping them identify their emotions. They might never admit it, but teens often need their parents' help identifying their emotions. Parents are usually better at recognizing their teens' feelings because they have lived longer and experienced more. Stepping up and helping this process with your teen by recognizing the signs and paying attention to their feelings is important. A teen whose parents recognize they're angry can learn to do the same for themselves. This identification helps teens describe their feelings without resorting to general terms like "bad" or "good" and can help them explore these feelings.

Next time you notice your teen is upset or angry, ask them, "What are you feeling?" and then follow up with, "What are you telling yourself about this situation?" Often, your teenager's thoughts about a situation are the most important for understanding their emotions. They might think, "I'm worthless," "Everyone hates me," or "I will never get better." These thoughts are uncomfortable. If your teen believes everyone hates them or has no control over their life, it's time to step in and make them step back to ask themselves, "Is this true?" Recognizing and clarifying your feelings is more than half the battle for building resilience.

Another way you can support your teen's resilience is by offering positive reinforcement and validating their feelings. Feelings are often divisive because one person thinks their child is "too sensitive" while another thinks they are "just fine." However, the truth about emotions is they are neither good nor bad; they merely exist. Acknowledging your teen's feelings and validating them as genuine helps them understand that their emotions are real and legitimate. Validation keeps them from beating themselves up for feeling a certain way and keeps them open to exploring how to make themselves feel better.

Supporting your teen's resilience also means you must support their ability to explore and question their reality. Allowing them to change their minds and make decisions is an important part of this process. Your teen will be more confident and capable if they can think for themselves and come to their own conclusions. Encouraging them to have opinions, explore viewpoints, and express their thoughts about a situation is vital for creating resilience. You will encourage your child to think critically and look at situations objectively rather than jumping to conclusions or following others blindly. By fostering a sense of autonomy, you empower them to take ownership of their decisions and actions, ultimately leading to personal growth and development. Mistakes and missteps are a natural part of life, so allowing your teen the space to make and learn from these mistakes will only strengthen their resilience. Resilience is hard work, requiring effort from all family members, not just teenagers. It helps if you prioritize supporting and trusting your child to come up with solutions for themselves.

Chapter 5: Emotional Regulation Training

In a world where emotions are often given little attention, it's tough for teens to learn how to manage their feelings and voice them constructively. Emotional regulation is learning to clear your head, relax your body, and focus on a task without getting sidetracked by emotions. Unfortunately, many teenagers feel lost in the daily emotional roller coaster. Emotions can move them quickly from happiness to anger to fear and cloud their judgment, making it hard to focus on schoolwork, friendships, or other important responsibilities. Outside help is needed.

What Is Emotional Regulation?

Everyone experiences emotions every day. Sometimes, they are mild, and other times, they're intense. Everyone's temperament is different, and so are the triggers for emotions. Some people are more easily angered than others. Some get anxious in crowds, but others feel energized by them. Some find happiness through music, while others need food to relax. Many are equally good at managing their emotions and are guided by their internal signals. However, for many teenagers, emotional responses to situations and interactions change depending on the day, where they are, who they are with, or their mood.

Good emotional regulation can help you calm down when you're upset.
https://www.pexels.com/photo/man-in-gray-long-sleeve-shirt-sitting-on-brown-wooden-chair-5255996/

Emotional regulation is recognizing an emotion as it happens, identifying it, understanding its meaning, and choosing how to react. It's not about repressing emotions or pretending they don't exist. It's about acknowledging them and managing them your way. Emotional regulation is a relatively new term but not a new idea. Everyone has felt the benefits of having good emotional regulation skills-for instance, calming down when you're upset, empathizing with others, and accepting change as part of life. For teenagers, learning to regulate their feelings can help with high stress, fluctuating hormones, and a growing sense that the world is a threatening place. Learning new ways to manage the emotional roller coaster allows them to stay calm and focused on situations causing anxiety, like speaking in front of groups, meeting new people, or giving presentations.

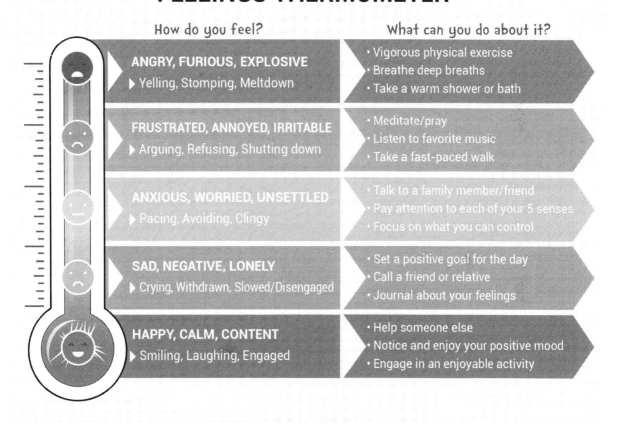

FEELINGS THERMOMETER

How do you feel?

What can you do about it?

ANGRY, FURIOUS, EXPLOSIVE
▶ Yelling, Stomping, Meltdown

- Vigorous physical exercise
- Breathe deep breaths
- Take a warm shower or bath

FRUSTRATED, ANNOYED, IRRITABLE
▶ Arguing, Refusing, Shutting down

- Meditate/pray
- Listen to favorite music
- Take a fast-paced walk

ANXIOUS, WORRIED, UNSETTLED
▶ Pacing, Avoiding, Clingy

- Talk to a family member/friend
- Pay attention to each of your 5 senses
- Focus on what you can control

SAD, NEGATIVE, LONELY
▶ Crying, Withdrawn, Slowed/Disengaged

- Set a positive goal for the day
- Call a friend or relative
- Journal about your feelings

HAPPY, CALM, CONTENT
▶ Smiling, Laughing, Engaged

- Help someone else
- Notice and enjoy your positive mood
- Engage in an enjoyable activity

Benefits of Emotional Regulation

Emotional regulation is different from "putting on a happy face." It's using your emotions daily to build relationships, help yourself when upset, and strengthen your resolve during challenges. It builds mental toughness and helps you be brave in facing your fears. However, the benefits aren't only emotional. Learning to deal with intense emotions builds self-reliance, helps you manage your anger, and teaches you to trust yourself so others are more inclined to trust you.

Teens with good emotional regulation skills are better equipped to deal with the ups and downs of daily drama, build positive relationships, handle stress, and deal with changes. Here are a few of the many benefits of emotional regulation:

1. **Improved Relationships:** With better self-control, teenagers can choose not to say the first thing that comes to their minds and avoid saying something hurtful in anger or frustration. They're better at voicing what they think. The more informed they are about themselves, the better their solution is when they're upset. When teenagers learn to manage their emotions healthily, instead of being reactive to strong emotions, it gives them control in emotionally charged situations. It lets them build good relationships by being honest about their feelings.

2. **Less Stress:** Having your way of handling strong emotions saves time and energy so you can focus on other things. When teens learn to manage stress healthily and constructively, they replace negative thoughts with positive ones and are less likely to fly off the handle or decide out of anger.

3. **Better Regulation of Moods:** Mood regulation is important for emotional regulation, but it's also different. Mood is a short-term cycle that shifts and changes naturally throughout the day. Emotions are reactions to situations and events. When teenagers learn to regulate their moods, especially when they are strong, they can better deal with them. When they feel bad about something, they don't get into a negativity and hopelessness spiral, as is often the case for teenagers with high stress.

4. **Greater Mental Toughness:** Emotional regulation is dealing with strong emotions from the inside out rather than suppressing them from the outside in. It helps develop mental toughness to overcome life's challenges and setbacks. When teenagers know how to control their emotions, they find it easier to keep moving forward when things change or they encounter problems or difficulties. It's harnessing their inner strength instead of letting their emotional reactions hold them back.

5. **Building Self-Trust:** Emotional regulation helps you become aware of yourself and your reactions. You become better at noticing your emotions as they change, knowing what caused the change and the options available for dealing with each situation. It cultivates self-confidence and self-trust in staying balanced even when stressed or overwhelmed.

6. **Less Anxiety:** Emotional regulation skills help teenagers deal with anxiety by helping them manage those strong emotions so they don't build into panic attacks. The same skills help them fight negative self-talk and set limits on their emotional responses. It allows them to accept change as part of life and see their strengths instead of weaknesses.

7. **Respect from Others:** When people see how well you can manage your emotions, they will more likely respect what you say and do. You'll more likely be taken seriously in school and during social interactions because you don't react impulsively. You can better compromise and work out solutions by knowing when to voice your concerns and when to let things flow.

Components of Emotional Regulation within DBT

Three components to emotional regulation, each building on the others, are:

1. Identifying and Labeling Emotions

The first step is understanding what you feel. You must identify and label your emotions, like mad, jealous, sad, happy, etc. It is the most basic emotional regulation skill, but it's the cornerstone for building the rest of your skills. You must learn to deal with your emotions; you can't do that if you don't know what they are.

2. Distinguishing between Thoughts and Feelings

The next step is distinguishing between thoughts and feelings - a shift in thinking because most people think of their emotions as thoughts. They differ; you must separate them if you want to manage your emotions.

You can better understand what's happening in your head when you can separate your thoughts from your feelings. It's easier to deal with a situation when you know why you're reacting a certain way and whether it is based on rational thoughts or purely emotional responses. Recognizing the distinction between thoughts and feelings gives you greater self-awareness and control over your emotional reactions. This self-awareness allows you to respond to situations deliberately rather than reacting impulsively based on fleeting emotions. Also, when you understand the underlying thoughts behind your feelings, you can uncover underlying beliefs or assumptions influencing your emotional responses. This observation allows you to challenge and reframe those thoughts, leading to healthier and more constructive emotional outcomes.

3. Reducing Vulnerability to Emotional Triggers

The final step of emotional regulation is learning to recognize and reduce your vulnerability to strong emotions. It means identifying and not giving in to triggers, causing you to lose control of your emotions, either through thought or action. For example, someone upset over an argument with a friend might be tempted to lash out at her parents because they seem like an easier target for expressing hostility. Similarly, a person experiencing anxiety about the future might withdraw from friends and family to avoid dealing with what they fear and feel uncomfortable with—the future. Recognizing these potential hot moments can help you take steps to avoid triggering a strong emotional response. It is easier when you have tools and strategies at your disposal. The DBT skills of distress tolerance provide the foundation for managing emotional vulnerability. They help you develop the resilience to overcome emotional triggers and remain strong when emotions run high.

Distress Tolerance Exercises for Teens

The Distress Tolerance skills in DBT are aimed at helping people, including teenagers, navigate difficult emotions and situations without resorting to harmful or impulsive behaviors. These skills are particularly beneficial for teens who experience heightened emotional sensitivity and struggle with managing intense feelings. By learning and practicing distress tolerance exercises, they can gain control over their emotions and develop healthier coping mechanisms.

These exercises range from simple breathing techniques to more complex strategies like distraction or self-soothing. As the parent, you'll guide your teenager through these exercises while also building your distress tolerance skills. Here are some common scenarios:

Handling Peer Pressure

Teens are often pressured into actions they know are wrong just to fit in with friends or schoolmates. It could be as simple as smoking in school with friends or, more importantly, lying to their parents about where they've been, skipping school, or stealing from a store. These situations are challenging for teens to navigate, as the pressure to fit in with friends and be part of a group can be intense. You can step in as a parent and help your teen develop distress tolerance skills to handle peer pressure situations.

Peer pressure may cause your teen to change their behavior.
https://www.pexels.com/photo/multiethnic-male-students-gossiping-about-sad-crying-woman-6147132/

For instance, a teenager is pressured into ditching classes with friends. This teenager can:

1. Use deep breathing exercises to calm themselves down and recognize they don't have to do something merely because their friends are.

2. They can use diffusion techniques (in this case, humor) to help them see the situation in a different light and not take their friends' pressure so seriously.

3. Another strategy would be to practice mindfulness—observing your thoughts, feelings, physical sensations, and actions without judging them as good or bad. Mindfulness helps the teen recognize they simply have the thought of ditching class because they perceive their friends want them to do it. There is no right or wrong decision at this moment, and as long as they are aware of the choice and know the consequences, they can choose to ditch class or not.

Managing Academic Stress

Students who struggle with academic failure often experience intense stress with setbacks or challenges in the classroom. This distress can lead to emotional reactions, causing them to shut down, act out, or even run away. Students can use the distress tolerance skills in DBT to help them manage these difficult feelings and allow themselves the space and time to get through an academic setback.

For example, a student who struggles with being overwhelmed by schoolwork could:

1. Use the breathing exercise to calm themselves down.

2. Using diffusion techniques, try to see the stressful situation from a different perspective.

3. Challenge their automatic thoughts by looking for evidence contradicting them. For example, they could use questioning skills to challenge the thought "I can't handle things at school" by listing why they can do things at school, like attending class, doing homework, and following teachers' instructions.

4. The next logical step is a mindfulness exercise to help them practice observing their thoughts and feelings without judging or fighting them. It can be as simple as sitting in a quiet room and paying attention to how they feel about school, taking note of their thoughts and feelings without responding or reacting to them.

Resolving Conflict with a Friend

As teenagers, they often have strong feelings about disagreeing with or being critical of their friends. It isn't easy to stand up for yourself against friends who share the same beliefs and are often supported by another group. Teens can use DBT distress tolerance skills to resolve conflict and maintain friendships with their mates while still retaining their beliefs and values.

For example, if a friend in their group is constantly criticizing a teen, they can:

1. Practice breathing exercises to help them calm down and stop their automatic fight-or-flight reaction.

2. Challenge their automatic thoughts by looking for evidence to see if they're right or wrong.

3. Distract themselves from their uncomfortable feelings by getting absorbed in something else, like listening to music or going for a walk.

4. Practice self-soothing exercises like taking a warm shower, listening to calming music, or playing with a stress ball to help release tension and frustration.

Progressive Muscle Relaxation for Teens and Parents

You and your child can find relief from overwhelming emotions by practicing progressive muscle relaxation together. This exercise involves intentionally tensing and then relaxing different muscle groups in the body, one at a time, to help recognize and manage physical sensations associated with stress and anxiety. It is an excellent technique to try when your child feels like their emotions are running wild and it's hard to get a grip, like when preparing for an exam, before a big game, or after a stressful day at school. Not only will this exercise help your child to deal with their emotions as healthily as they can, but it also can be used as a tool to help you better understand how you can support your child's emotional regulation. To begin:

1. **Step one:** Find a cozy, quiet, and relaxing place to lie or sit down.

2. **Step two:** Start with the toes and tense them for five seconds, then relax them. Move up to the calves, then the thighs, until you get to the face. This will go more smoothly if you don't get caught up in particular muscle groups per se – just on the different parts of the body. By consciously tensing and relaxing each area, your child can bring awareness to their physical sensations and learn to differentiate between tension and relaxation.

3. **Step three:** As you move through each body part, encourage your child to pay attention to how each area feels when it is tense versus when it is relaxed. Are there any differences in temperature, pressure, or other sensations? By tuning into these subtle changes, your child can develop a deeper understanding of their body's response to stress and anxiety.

4. **Step four:** Once your child has gone through all the muscle groups, guide them to take a few deep breaths. Remember, your goal here is not to rid yourself of all anxiety but to learn how to manage it. As your child becomes more aware of how their body reacts to stress and anxiety, they can begin to adjust their behavior and reactions accordingly.

Emotional distress can tremendously impact teenagers' health, especially when external triggers like bullying, peer pressure, or frustration with school set it off. DBT teaches teens to manage and resolve their emotional discomfort and to tolerate their feelings and thoughts without giving in to destructive urges. This skill can be learned over time and sustained through practice. After learning it, teens will be better equipped to handle their emotions, learn from their mistakes, and lead happier, healthier lives.

Chapter 6: Teaching Your Teen to Weather the Storm

Parenting a teenager . . . it may feel like they have been struggling with one emotional storm after another. Between the raging hormones, questions about their sexuality, and a general struggle with fitting in, even their most minor problems are challenging. For adults experiencing the same challenges and emotions, your teen's struggles can seem like a nightmare. Fortunately, there is an approach that has been shown to help families manage these powerful storms without them turning into hurricanes.

While your teen struggles with trust, self-worth, and identity issues, they will also have tests on social skills, asserting themselves, and managing emotions. These tests can be exhausting for teenagers and lead them to avoid situations and people they need, i.e., you. It can become an escalating problem; truth be told, these storms are not what you need. An angry teen is a teen who is not communicating with you, which can become a barrier in your relationship. The stress of these storms will cause more tension with your teen than you realize; your job is to lighten the load. Your child needs to learn to weather these storms and communicate with you healthily for all parties.

Introducing Distress Tolerance

Distress Tolerance (DT) is a skill that helps your teen navigate the tricky waters of these emotional storms and improves their communication. It teaches them to tolerate difficult emotions and situations without resorting to destructive behaviors. By teaching your teen distress tolerance skills, you help them develop healthier coping mechanisms and a more rewarding relationship with you. It's like having a practical survival guide for your teen's emotional world.

Distress tolerance skills are simple to teach but can be extremely difficult to master. They take practice, commitment, and learning from mistakes. Distress tolerance focuses on learning the skills rather than the outcome. The outcome is your teen handling these situations better. However, the process is the important part. The process allows you both to talk about issues and work together to make things more manageable. The only downside is the struggle to master the skills. But on the bright side, the struggle is a sign that the skill is being learned.

Four basic skills teach distress tolerance: cognitive restructuring, distraction, self-soothing, and acceptance. Each skill can be taught separately, but the key to mastery is knowing when to use them.

Cognitive Restructuring

Cognitive restructuring is reframing situations that are perceived to react to them better. It might sound simple, but it is incredibly difficult. The first step is identifying your "hot thoughts," which are the thoughts that come to mind when you are emotional. These hot thoughts often contain irrational beliefs or negative self-talk, fueling emotional distress. Once you have identified these hot thoughts, the next step is to challenge and replace them with more realistic and positive thoughts. This process requires self-awareness, mindfulness, and a willingness to challenge your thinking patterns.

Cognitive restructuring is an incredible tool to help break free from negative thinking cycles and develop a more balanced and rational mindset. It takes practice and patience, but there is something to be said for learning to think differently. Actively challenging and replacing negative thoughts shifts your perspective and creates a more positive and empowering mindset. This process involves questioning the evidence and validity of hot thoughts and considering alternative explanations and perspectives. Remember, thoughts are not facts; merely because you think something doesn't mean it's true. Through cognitive restructuring, you recognize and challenge the distorted thinking patterns tossed into your mind and replace those patterns with clearer, more productive ones.

Main Points

- Identify your hot thoughts
- Reframe them using concrete evidence
- Develop a positive, realistic outlook

Distraction Techniques

It's important to distract yourself when feeling anxious or frustrated.
https://unsplash.com/photos/bwKtz4YVtmA?utm_source=unsplash&utm_medium=referral&utm_content=creditShareLink

Distraction techniques are a potent way to subdue overwhelming emotions. They are particularly useful in certain situations to help you distract yourself from thought spirals or negative self-talk. These techniques can be effective for almost any emotion but are most effective for anger or anxiety. When you become anxious or angry, your body reacts so that you feel out of control and overwhelmed - your breathing changes, your heart races, and you think about the worst possible outcome. As these feelings mount, your body becomes more agitated and emotional. In this state of mind, thinking rationally or calmly about anything is nearly impossible because emotions take precedence over rational thought. Distraction techniques are useful when this happens. These techniques are easy to learn and simple to apply during a crisis or tense situation. They can help you calm down, cool off, and regain control. A few examples of distraction techniques include deep breathing, counting backward, listening to music, or thinking about something else entirely. These techniques won't make the situation go away, but they can help you regain clarity and perspective.

Main Points

- Breathe slowly and deeply
- Focus on an object or color around you
- Move your body to calm yourself down
- Do something to distract you

Self-Soothing

Self-soothing is providing comfort and reassurance to yourself when upset or in pain. It recognizes your discomfort in a tough situation and finds ways to make yourself feel better. It is difficult to know how to fix it when you are very upset or agitated. Self-soothing is not about fixing anything; it is about learning to tolerate and feel comfortable in that moment. Whether through deep breathing, softly running your fingers through your hair, or thinking about something that makes you happy, this skill teaches your teen to recognize when they need comfort and provide it for themselves. Finding ways to relax and calm down can be a much-needed outlet in tense situations. Self-soothing techniques are particularly useful when negative emotions won't go away. Even if the situation intensifies, self-soothing can help you feel more at ease, in control, and confident that you can handle it.

Main Points

- Learn ways to calm yourself down
- Make sure you make time for yourself to feel better
- Comfort yourself when you need it most

Acceptance

Acceptance is a powerful skill because it teaches letting go of expectations and understanding that things won't always go how you want them to. It is being comfortable in situations that are often uncomfortable. Maybe your daughter doesn't get into her first-choice school, or your son breaks up with his first girlfriend. It does not mean something is wrong; it means that life is perfectly imperfect. As humans, you expect everything to go your way and have unrealistic expectations of others and circumstances. However, acceptance teaches you to be more realistic and patient with life's situations to move forward with a clearer head.

When you accept how things are or how other people act, it creates more room for you to grow and thrive. Unfortunately, often, you make decisions based on expectations rather than reality. You create a blueprint for disaster. You decide based on an unrealistic understanding of the world and people, leading to unhappiness, disappointment, and resentment when expectations are not met. If more teenagers could learn about the power of acceptance, it would be a huge step toward ensuring the next generation of adults are well-adjusted, happy, and functioning society members. Acceptance might not solve every issue in their lives, but it can make each day more enjoyable and rewarding.

Main Points

- Be realistic in your expectations
- Be patient with yourself
- Learn to accept those around you for who they are
- Do not assume you know what other people are thinking and feeling
- Be happy with the way things are

Coping Skills Toolbox (For Teens)

This is a special activity to help your teenager develop self-awareness and figure out what they need to deal with their emotions in various scenarios. If you have a very young teenager, you might need to help them with this activity as they won't have many coping skills at their disposal. Coping skills are your way of handling life's challenges. It's what you do to get through difficult situations, including drawing, writing, exercising, journaling, or talking it out. Think of them as little helpers holding you together when things get tough. Everyone has different coping skills, so this activity teaches your teenager to discover what helps them and when it is best to use them.

To create a coping skills toolbox, you will need to:

1. Get a box, some paper, and a pen.
2. Decorate your box with stickers in unique shapes and colors, or cut out pictures from magazines or posters to glue onto the box.
3. On your paper, write down a few scenarios where you are frustrated, sad, or upset - one scenario per paper.
4. Label each piece of paper with at least three coping skills you think will work in this situation. It can be anything from talking to someone to writing a letter or distracting yourself. The list can be as long as you want, but each coping skill must be healthy, positive, and constructive.
5. Once you have listed your coping skills and scenarios, put them in the box.
6. Look through the box for an appropriate response or coping skill when you're in a tough situation.

99 Coping Skills

1. Exercise (running, walking, etc.).
2. Put on fake tattoos.
3. Write (poetry, stories, journal).
4. Scribble/doodle on paper.
5. Be with other people.
6. Watch a favorite TV show.
7. Post on web boards, and answer others' posts.
8. Go see a movie.
9. Do a wordsearch or crossword.
10. Do schoolwork.
11. Play a musical instrument.
12. Paint your nails, do your make-up or hair.
13. Sing.
14. Study the sky.
15. Punch a punching bag.
16. Cover yourself with Band-Aids where you want to cut.
17. Let yourself cry.
18. Take a nap (only if you are tired).
19. Take a hot shower or relaxing bath.
20. Play with a pet.
21. Go shopping.
22. Clean something.
23. Knit or sew.
24. Read a good book.
25. Listen to music.
26. Try some aromatherapy (candle, lotion, room spray).
27. Meditate.
28. Go somewhere very public.
29. Bake cookies.
30. Alphabetize your CDs/DVDs/books.
31. Paint or draw.
32. Rip paper into itty-bitty pieces
33. Shoot hoops, kick a ball.
34. Write a letter or send an email.
35. Plan your dream room (colors/furniture).
36. Hug a pillow or stuffed animal.
37. Hyperfocus on something like a rock, hand, etc.
38. Dance.
39. Make hot chocolate, milkshake or smoothie.
40. Play with modeling clay or PlayDough.
41. Build a pillow fort.
42. Go for a nice, long drive.
43. Complete something you've been putting off.
44. Draw on yourself with a marker.
45. Take up a new hobby.
46. Look up recipes, cook a meal.
47. Look at pretty things, like flowers or art.
48. Create or build something.
49. Pray.
50. Make a list of blessings in your life.
51. Read the Bible.
52. Go to a friend's house.
53. Jump on a trampoline.
54. Watch an old, happy movie.
55. Contact a hotline/ your therapist.
56. Talk to someone close to you.
57. Ride a bicycle.
58. Feed the ducks, birds, or squirrels.
59. Color with Crayons.
60. Memorize a poem, play, or song.
61. Stretch.
62. Search for ridiculous things on the internet.
63. "Shop" on-line (without buying anything).
64. Color-coordinate your wardrobe.
65. Watch fish.
66. Make a CD/playlist of your favorite songs.
67. Play the "15 minute game." (Avoid something for 15 minutes, when time is up start again.)
68. Plan your wedding/prom/other event.
69. Plant some seeds.
70. Hunt for your perfect home or car on-line.
71. Try to make as many words out of your full name as possible.
72. Sort through your photographs.
73. Play with a balloon.
74. Give yourself a facial.
75. Find yourself some toys and play.
76. Start collecting something.
77. Play video/computer games.
78. Clean up trash at your local park.
79. Perform a random act of kindness for someone.
80. Text or call an old friend.
81. Write yourself an "I love you because..." letter.
82. Look up new words and use them.
83. Rearrange furniture.
84. Write a letter to someone that you may never send.
85. Smile at least five people.
86. Play with little kids.
87. Go for a walk (with or without a friend).
88. Put a puzzle together.
89. Clean your room /closet.
90. Try to do handstands, cartwheels, or backbends.
91. Yoga.
92. Teach your pet a new trick.
93. Learn a new language.
94. Move EVERYTHING in your room to a new spot.
95. Get together with friends and play Frisbee, soccer or basketball.
96. Hug a friend or family member.
97. Search on-line for new songs/artists.
98. Make a list of goals for the week/month/year/5 years.
99. Face paint.

This activity can explore various coping skills your child might not know they have or help teens determine the best skill in different situations. It is a great activity to use initially when your child has no experience with certain strategies. As they develop coping skills, the box can be improved and updated.

The Value of Validation

Teens want to be accepted for who they are and what they do but often don't know how to tell you. It is human nature and is something parents should be aware of and sensitive to. As parents, you must create an environment where your teenager feels validated and understood. Validating their emotions and experiences helps them feel heard and fosters trust and open communication within the parent-child relationship.

Teens often feel different things in various situations. Sometimes, they have strong emotions they wish to share with you. Other times, they don't know how to handle them or what to say to you. Sometimes, they become very happy and excited and want to share the good news; other times, they are sad, angry, or scared and don't want you to know about it. They are learning to cope with their emotions, deal with situations, and navigate relationships every day. You must provide a space where your teenager knows what they feel is valid and important, even if it does not match your opinion or expectations.

If you don't know where to start, these validatory sentences might help:

- "I'm so proud of you."
- "What a great idea."
- "That sounds hard."
- "I'm sorry that happened."
- "You've handled the situation very well. I'm proud of how you reacted."
- "You've done very well so far. Keep at it."
- "You are right."

Validation should not be used as an attempt to avoid the emotional storm. Many parents are too afraid of being honest and saying the wrong thing. They try to avoid difficult situations for their teen by preemptively coddling or telling them everything will be fine when it isn't. Unfortunately, these tactics often backfire and only create more issues for your teenager. It might seem counterintuitive, but avoiding difficult situations is a classic symptom of overprotection and over-parenting (yes, there is such a thing). Avoidance can turn into anger and resentment in your teen. It teaches them that you do not trust them to make good decisions, think for themselves, and handle things on their own. It creates a sense of helplessness and hopelessness, leading to low self-esteem, depression, and rebellious behavior.

Instead, help them navigate this natural stage in their development by providing the tools to succeed and grow. Let them know you trust them and will always be there to guide them while giving them the space to experience these changes independently. They haven't always been the person they are now. They used to depend on you for everything, but now they are growing into adults and learning about the outside world for themselves. Give them room to fly, help them when they need it most, and trust their abilities.

Key Takeaways

- Teens are growing up and experiencing the full range of emotions and situations they will encounter as adults. It is natural for them to be actively engaged in their emotional growth.

- Don't avoid difficult situations or want your teenager to feel differently about them. Do not try to 'cuddle' them out of a tough situation when there is room for growth instead.

- Let your teen know you still love them, even when they are having a hard time.

- Don't pass up an opportunity to tell your teenager you are proud of them, even if their choices differ from yours.

- Open communication is essential for trust and honesty in your relationship.

- Remember to validate feelings and the person, not the behavior or choice.

Chapter 7: Encouraging Interpersonal Relations

Sometimes, it feels like all children want to do these days is seclude themselves with their phones and computers. Social media and other online communication have significantly reduced the time people spend face-to-face, making it harder for teenagers to build interpersonal relationships to thrive in an increasingly complex social environment.

However, building healthy interpersonal relationships is not only important for children who want to succeed in school and life; it's essential for everyone because forming strong relationships is the most reliable indicator of a person's overall mental health and stability. Healthy relationships help people look at the world through rose-colored glasses and cope with stress, anxiety, and daily drama. Several studies have found that healthy relationships can help manage many serious mental health conditions.

Yet, forming and maintaining healthy relationships hasn't always been considered a priority in schools, where they are more likely to be viewed as an obstacle than a solution. But now, more schools recognize that building strong relationships between students can better prepare them for the future and develop a stronger sense of belonging to a community.

Building strong relationships can prepare your teens for the future.
https://unsplash.com/photos/jCEpN62oWLA?utm_source=unsplash&utm_medium=referral&utm_content=creditShareLink

Building healthy relationships with one another also needs to happen at home. More importantly, it should begin at home. It should be modeled and encouraged, and young people must be taught to put their best foot forward. However, it can also be challenging for parents to know how to support their children in this area. What does building a healthy relationship with your teenager even look like? How do you even begin to start?

For many teens, a positive relationship with their parents is not a priority. But imagine if they found out those seemingly mundane interactions with their parents have the power to shape their future irreversibly and permanently. How would that change how they think about relationships in general? How would it change what they think of you?

Nurturing healthy relationships is the essence of human interaction. It's what gives the confidence to take on new challenges and opportunities. It is what allows you to bounce back from hard times. Teenagers especially need this skill. They need it to succeed in school and life and to find social support should things go awry in their future.

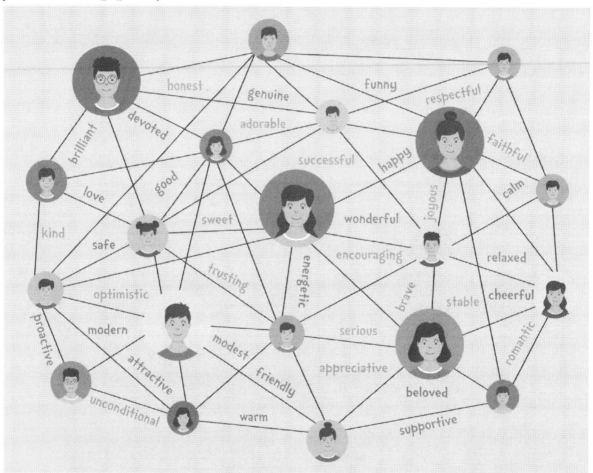

So, how can parents encourage this skill in their teenagers without losing them in the process? How can they encourage this skill that could last a lifetime and might determine whether their children are happy or miserable for the rest of their lives? The key is embracing the effective teaching approach. Like any skill, relationship building with your teens can be taught, modeled, and encouraged. The best part about learning about relationships is that it's a lot of fun. It involves storytelling and bonding, and as long as it's done with love and respect, your teen won't feel compelled to hide in their room.

Building Healthy Relationships at Home

The human brain is an amazing organ. It can detect patterns and predict outcomes, even when those outcomes aren't always completely predictable. If you know how to induce and maximize this ability in your teenager, you can use their natural inclination for prediction to your advantage. You can encourage your child to think about the future and then take action from that thinking. For example, what's the first thing you might do if you want your teenager to do well in school? Get them to study, right? It sounds simple, but what if your teen doesn't want to study? What if they'd rather be out playing? What if they'd rather be on Instagram?

As you can imagine, forcing your teenager to study for one hour a night is a recipe for trouble, but if you ask them to structure their days to maximize their study time, it becomes much more interesting. Suddenly, they're in control of the entire process and know they will get what they want precisely, but you know they're getting what they need. It's a win-win situation, so it's easy to see why teens want to get on board with the idea.

This is only one way to leverage the natural inclination for prediction to your advantage. You can use this same thinking for healthy relationships at home, too. You cannot force your teen into having a healthy relationship with you. They must take ownership of their decision, and the result will be more successful if they believe in it. It's important that they feel they're making choices so they can look back on them and feel good about their decisions and the opportunities they created.

You need to devise ways for your teen to practice and perfect their skills in interpersonal relationships. Provide them with opportunities like a chance to pick the restaurant to grab lunch or plan the next family trip. Not only can you use this opportunity to practice their negotiation skills, but it also gives them a chance to hone their interpersonal skills in a setting more forgiving than the real world. These opportunities give your teen the space to think about how they interact with others and what role they want to play in the world.

Common Challenges Teens Face When Forming and Maintaining Relationships

How you and your teen relate to one another can directly impact how they develop a sustainable sense of self. At such a young age, they often search for their identity and try to figure out who they are, what kind of person they want to be, and how they think they should act. This search is not easy for any young person, but it can be made more difficult for several reasons.

Some common challenges teens face when forming and maintaining relationships include:

1. Peer Pressure

Peer pressure is a challenge most teens face daily, but it's one that not all are equipped to deal with. Some teens can walk away from a situation where they're being pressured to act against their morals or beliefs. Others may not. The best way to prepare your teen for the real world is by teaching them about the dangers of peer pressure from a young age. They might feel the need to conform to fit in with their peers, even if it means compromising their values and desires. Peer pressure can greatly impact teenagers' ability to form and maintain healthy relationships as they become surrounded by people who do things they're uncomfortable with. This constant struggle between fitting in and staying true to themselves can create a significant barrier to building meaningful connections with others.

2. Self-Doubt

The root cause of all negative thoughts and feelings is self-doubt. When you doubt yourself, you look at your surroundings suspiciously, resulting in distrust of others and a lack of trust in yourself. It becomes challenging or impossible to form meaningful relationships. So, teach your child from a young age about the importance of self-esteem and developing healthy self-awareness to curb this obstacle.

3. Lack of Self-Awareness

In this era of social media, it's easier than ever to get caught up in the demands of the internet and lose track of who you are. Your teen might be more susceptible to feeling isolated or left out from the world around them, resulting in a greater need to be accepted by others and a lower likelihood of being honest about themselves. Encourage your child to practice honesty with themselves and accept who they are by finding interests that appeal to them and pursuing hobbies to learn even more about themselves.

4. Social Anxiety

Social anxiety is more common than you might realize. Nearly 30% of adolescents have reported experiencing social anxiety. It can make it difficult for your teen to relate to others and lead to disconnection from the rest of the world. Recognize your child's social anxiety signs and provide them with sound support. Encourage them to engage in social activities, but also respect their boundaries and give them space when needed. Understanding and supporting your child's emotional reactions helps them build confidence to feel comfortable approaching others and forming relationships.

These obstacles don't need to be permanent barriers to your child's ability to form healthy relationships with you and others. By identifying them early, you can better understand how your child interacts with the world and how you can help them open up more and feel comfortable in their skin.

How to Help Your Teen Build Their Social Skills

Just like any other skill, social skills must be practiced and perfected if they are going to be effective. However, social skills are a bit different in that they only grow and change as the individual does. The social world is complex and ever-changing, so your teen must be able to adapt quickly and easily to keep up. The social skills your teen develops now will follow them throughout their life, so you need to develop a plan for helping them grow their skills from the very beginning. These are some common ways you can help with this:

- Understand your child's interests:

Socializing can often be much easier for some children than it is for others. The key to building their social skills is to pick up on what aspects of the social world they find most interesting. Does your child love animals? Introduce them to a local animal shelter and the volunteers that work there. Do they enjoy watching movies? Set up a movie night at home with their friends. Are they interested in sports or music? Engage with them over these topics through conversations, allowing them to share more about themselves.

- Be a great listener:

One overlooked aspect of being a good parent is letting your teen do the talking. Most people are comfortable talking about themselves, so allow your teen to do this. Pay attention to what they say and how they say it. This will make it easier for you to understand them on a deeper level and prepare you to help them develop their social skills in ways that appeal to who they are as a person.

- **Provide opportunities for new experiences:**

Children developing their social skills need new experiences to keep their learning process fresh and exciting. If your teen can't get out much or doesn't have opportunities to expand their social circle, find ways for them to meet new people through things like volunteering, taking part in school clubs and sports teams, or getting involved with other extracurricular activities. This will provide them with new experiences and encourage them to continue trying new things to find what they enjoy.

- **Encourage socialization:**

Encourage your teen to engage in healthy social activities through monthly events or even by having them join a club at school. This may take some getting used to, but it will help them develop their skills and feel more comfortable with others. Once they've gotten the hang of things, encourage them to make new friends and find ways to implement their skills into their socializing process.

- **Encourage a positive mindset:**

A negative mindset can make it extremely difficult for your child to feel confident and comfortable in social situations. Encourage them to embrace their uniqueness, find things they have in common with others, and remember that everyone has things they are good at or enjoy. When they are more self-aware of themselves and the habits that make them unique, they will begin to see themselves as capable people who bring value to the world around them.

Role-Playing DBT Game for Parents and Teens

This game should be played with your teenager. It is a fun way to teach them to identify their difficulty in expressing their thoughts, feelings, and goals. The game is very simple: pick a scenario and ask your teen four questions:

1. Do you have a problem? (Identifying their difficulty).
2. How do you feel? (Expressing their feelings).
3. How do you want to feel? (Listing their goal or wish).
4. Do you have an idea how to get there? (Describing how they will achieve the goal or wish).

Use their answers to assess, discuss, and plan a strategy for change. The questions are basic, so you can tailor them to your teenager's specific situation. You can play the game as much as you want and for as long as is necessary.

Examples of situations that could trigger a response in your teenager:

1. Your teenager is shy and doesn't interact well with people.
2. Your teenager has anxiety and doesn't want to participate in group activities because they're too intense.
3. Your teenager has many friends and is worried you don't like them.
4. Your teenager has trouble making friends at school because they're not assertive enough to get what they want from the relationship (i.e., wanting to be their friend, not being teased for not being popular, etc.).
5. Your teenager is ashamed of their body and uncomfortable with their sexual orientation, gender identity, or sexual activity.
6. Your teenager is angry because they think no one listens to their thoughts and feelings.

You know your child best and know what situations are most relevant. These are only a few examples of what could evoke an emotional response from a teenager. When doing this activity, encourage your teen to stick to I-statements, use emotional expression, and find a way to say what they want without attacking the other person. It allows them to thoroughly explore their feelings and why they feel that way.

Interpersonal Effectiveness within DBT

Dealing with relationships can be tricky. In an ideal world, you'd like to make every situation go smoothly, and your child would never have a problem being honest or making good decisions. But unfortunately, that's not how the world works, so you have to work with what you have; what you have is a teenager.

Three important skills must be applied when dealing with any relationship: empathy, assertive communication, and boundaries. The aim is to ensure your teenager is being true to themselves without hurting others and allowing others to be true to themselves.

Here's how each of these skills can help you achieve this:

1. Empathy

Empathy can be defined in many ways, but it's easiest to think of it as understanding what the other person is feeling and going through. When we're empathetic, we understand other points of view and can take their perspective of feelings and emotions.

When you're empathetic, you listen to your child, ask open-ended questions, and focus on their concerns. When your teen is empathetic, they can ask questions and express their wants and needs without making anyone uncomfortable. Since empathy is such a powerful skill, it can make a substantial difference in the quality of your relationship. A good way to show your teen how effective empathy can be is to model it yourself. By showing them you can put yourself in their shoes and understand their perspective, they'll better understand how real and important empathy is.

2. Assertive Communication

Assertion can be broken down into two parts: expressing yourself and being respectful. These might seem contradictory, but they go hand in hand. When you're assertive, you're not throwing around emotional attacks or insults; you're showing the other person you're worthy of their respect by being clear about what you want to happen and why. When you're assertive, your child will understand consent and be more willing to recognize when someone crosses a boundary or gets out of line.

When assertive, they can voice their wants and needs without guilt or hesitation. They can also do this without hurting anyone else's feelings or making them uncomfortable or ashamed. A good strategy for teaching your teen assertiveness is to lead by example. Show them how to communicate effectively and assertively by using "I" statements, clearly expressing their needs and boundaries, and actively listening to others. Encourage open and honest conversations and validate their feelings and opinions. Teach them the importance of respecting others' boundaries and finding a balance between assertiveness and empathy.

3. Boundaries

Boundaries are a great way to protect yourself from feeling uncomfortable, guilty, or ashamed. Teenagers with good boundaries can say "no" to things without feeling bad or backing down. They will also use boundaries to prevent peer pressure and conformity.

A good way for your teen to understand the importance of boundaries is by teaching them the difference between healthy and unhealthy relationships. Healthy boundaries in relationships are focused on communication and how well you get along with others. Unhealthy boundaries are about conforming to social norms, accepting abusive behavior, and not having a voice in the relationship. When you set boundaries, you take control of your life and refuse to settle for unhealthy relationships.

Many things can make a relationship healthy or unhealthy, but respect is one of the biggest determining factors. A healthy relationship will respect your boundaries no matter what they are (unless the boundaries are unhealthy, but that's for another time). Dealing with someone who doesn't respect your boundaries can be intensely frustrating and emotionally draining, and no parent wants their child to go through it, especially at such a young age. But if you take the time to teach your child about healthy versus unhealthy relationships, you'll have a better chance of helping them understand and avoid them.

Chapter 8: Bridging the Gap Between You and Your Teenager

Whether a parent, an aunt, or a well-meaning friend shoved into the parenting arena by need or circumstance, you know that children can be tough to handle, especially when dealing with a teenager. They seem so different and untouchable at times – as if they've gone through a weird metamorphosis as they age. It's like you can never reach them, and they don't want to be seen with you. Luckily, there are ways to repair the rift between you and your teen, no matter how large.

There are many ways to bridge the gap between you and your teen.
https://unsplash.com/photos/2gYsZUmockw?utm_source=unsplash&utm_medium=referral&utm_content=creditShareLink

Here are some strategies to get started:

1. **Expand Your Horizons:** Feeling defensive when your teenager is acting out and you can't reach them is totally normal. Initially, it's easy to see yourself as the "bad guy," like you've done something wrong or they don't like you. However, step back and expand your horizons a little. For example, sometimes you're right, but they're not wrong either. They're merely acting their age, and that's perfectly OK. Ask yourself, "Is it really my fault my teenager doesn't want to talk to me?" If the answer is no, you're digging too deep and need a break so you both can breathe.

2. **You Don't Have to Be Best Friends:** This can be hard to swallow, but sometimes teenagers 'just don't care.' It doesn't mean you're a failure as a parent or there's something wrong with your teenager. They are teens and don't always want to talk to Mom or Dad when they get home from school. Let things lie; it won't hurt so much when they don't come looking for advice. Instead of getting angry at how little attention they pay you, practice active listening and non-judgmental communication when they do talk to you.

3. **Make Them Feel Important:** Even when your teenager isn't talking to you, they still need to feel important. You can say, "I'm glad we got to spend some time together today," or "It's good to see you smile." Teenagers need attention, even when it doesn't seem like they do. When they're ready to open up and let you in, you'll be glad you spent the extra time working on the relationship.

4. **Replace Negativity with Positivity:** Converse with your teenager to help them feel better about themselves. Sometimes just hearing you say or do something nice to them is all they need to get over the hump. Even if you don't know what's wrong, saying "I love you" at the end of a conversation is enough.

5. **Ask for Their Help Sometimes:** Before you know it, you'll have talked your teenager into dropping their defenses when you ask for help. You might be surprised at how well they listen to you and how willing they are to do their part to fix whatever is wrong. When your teenager cares about you and tries to help, they can be as sweet as when they were little children.

6. **Focus on the Fact That You Love Them:** No matter how big the rift is between you, remember you love them, and they love you. Let that be your light in the dark.

7. **Be There When the Moment Is Right:** Try connecting with your teenager after a rough day. When they open up to you, ensure to validate their feelings—not by pretending like you know how they feel, but by listening and sympathizing with their situation. This moment is when you can tell them you're happy to be there for them and that you'll always want to help them if needed.

8. **Be Friendly When You See Them:** Be friendly if your teenager needs a little space but talks to you anyway. Remember, sometimes teenagers fight with their parents because they don't feel they can talk to them, or when they do, the conversation isn't always pleasant. Ask yourself if it's worth losing your relationship over a few sarcastic comments and a few angry words. If the answer is no, try to understand your teenager's tough exterior more.

9. **Focus on the Positive:** Sometimes positive things happen in your family even though you can't see them. Maybe you got a new job (and your teenager was happy for you), or a friend is getting married (and your teenager is excited to be invited). Point these things out to your teen instead of focusing on their complaints. When you get a chance to focus on the positive, it's easier for you both.

10. **Respect Them:** Ultimately, respect makes your family work as a whole. When you respect your teenager, they'll respect you back. It's a two-way street, and it'll make you both feel much better. Instead of trying to get your teenager to behave a certain way, respect their differences; it's more important than being close or even best friends with them.

11. **Be Open to Compromise:** It might seem a little unusual to some, but you should accept compromise as part of your parenting strategy. You shouldn't want them to do everything your way because you'll never accomplish it. Instead, converse about what you both want and how far you can go. Let them know they're still their own person, which makes them special. Compromises work better than yelling and arguing over something small 90% of the time.

12. **Know How to Pick Your Battles:** Sometimes, you can win the argument, but it's not worth it. You might want to stand your ground or fight until the end, but avoiding a good old-fashioned shouting match is better for your relationship. When in doubt, choose the path of least resistance. Your family will be happier, and you might save yourself a few gray hairs.

Now you know what to do when your teenager doesn't want to talk. Be there for them when they're ready, but don't push too hard and become hostile. Instead, try the strategies above and list the things you love about your teen. When they feel comfortable enough to have a conversation, remember it's still about them, not you. Regardless of how bad things get between you, remember, they're still your baby.

Friendship-Building Exercises for Parents and Teens

- **Spooky Scavenger Hunt:** To get the blood pumping on Halloween night, host a spooky scavenger hunt for teams of parents and teens. Get a third party to hide an object or objects in different locations around the neighborhood or even inside the house. Then, all the parents and teens can go on an ultimate search through the neighborhood or house, following the clues and exchanging hints to find the hidden treasures. This activity not only promotes teamwork and problem-solving skills but also provides an opportunity for parents and teens to bond and have fun together. As you and your child work together to unravel the clues, you'll have the chance to communicate, strategize, and celebrate small victories along the way. Plus, the thrill of the hunt will create lasting memories and strengthen the connection between you and your child.

- **Cooking Challenge:** Another great activity for parents and teens to bond over is a cooking challenge. This fun and interactive experience allows you and your teen to showcase your culinary skills and creativity in the kitchen. Whether you choose to follow a recipe or create your own dish from scratch, the cooking challenge will provide a platform for you and your child to spend time together, problem-solve, and learn new cooking techniques. Not only will you create delicious meals (hopefully), but you will also gain a sense of accomplishment and pride in your culinary creations. From brainstorming recipe ideas to shopping for ingredients to finally presenting your dishes, every step of the cooking challenge will be filled with laughter, teamwork, and a healthy dose of friendly competition.

Chapter 9: The Family DBT Approach

A family in DBT is not necessarily a nuclear family of a mom, dad, and two children. It can be any collection of people sharing a relationship with one another and sharing responsibilities for caring for one another. Families include the relationships between parents and children, siblings, grandparents and grandchildren, and friends – any relationship with shared responsibility.

Family includes the relationships between parents, children, siblings, and grandparents.
https://unsplash.com/photos/L203i9Xi_XE

The family unit is one of the most complex systems to approach in therapy. It is a huge system that includes different relationships, each with its component of emotion regulation, communication, and relational rules to be managed. DBT recognizes this complexity and looks at everything from a systemic perspective. Hence, any changes made within the system must be done with consideration for how they will impact the whole system, not only one individual in the system.

Emotions between family members affect everyone, sometimes with lasting effects. These emotions can be expressed in many ways, including intense arguments, manipulation, passive aggressiveness, or avoidance. When a family member has an issue with anxiety or other emotional dysregulation, their behaviors can significantly impact others in the system. These effects can easily go unnoticed and be passed from one member to another without anyone necessarily realizing it's happening.

Dealing with emotions as a unit can make it easier for people to identify what is happening in a family and understand where their behaviors fit in a larger picture rather than seeing their behavior as an isolated event or issue. DBT's validation concept recognizes the importance of understanding how behavior impacts others and making an effort to treat people with the respect and humanity they deserve.

Validation takes another person's perspective and shows them you understand and believe them. It uses reflective listening skills to demonstrate understanding of the other person's thoughts, feelings, wants, and needs without necessarily judging or criticizing their actions or statements. This approach is used in many counseling sessions, from individual to group and family therapy.

Family DBT

Family DBT has the same core principles as individual dialectical behavior therapy, but the approach differs. Family DBT emphasizes what behavior family members exhibit in a situation rather than identifying specific dysfunctional behaviors. For example, instead of focusing on specific dysfunctional behaviors and suggesting how they could be changed, family DBT focuses on improving communication and problem-solving skills within the family unit. This approach recognizes that dysfunctional behavior within a family often results from poor communication patterns and unresolved conflicts. Family DBT aims to create a more supportive and harmonious family environment by addressing these underlying issues. It can involve teaching family members effective communication techniques, conflict-resolution strategies, and mindfulness skills.

Family DBT is different from individual DBT since it specifically focuses on how to act as a family and how to treat each other. It recognizes that how people function within a family often differs from how they function outside the family unit. Therefore, it requires a different approach to make the necessary changes.

Family-Oriented Activities for DBT

One of the main focuses of family DBT is to create a positive and supportive family environment so members can function well together. For this reason, family DBT sessions must be structured to encourage and promote communication and group cohesion.

Family DBT participants will engage in family-oriented activities as part of this therapy. These activities could be verbal or physical and possibly include homework assignments. If it does include homework assignments, they must have clear expectations and measurable goals. For example, family members might work on developing better interpersonal skills by role-playing scenarios where they practice new communication methods by listening, validating, and accepting each other's thoughts and feelings. These activities allow family members to demonstrate their understanding of each other's perspectives and communicate what they learned.

Some activities to try in a family DBT session include:

1. **Mindfulness Sessions:** These sessions use a guided meditation where family members sit in a circle and focus on the positive aspects of their relationships by recognizing each other's positive traits. Alternatively, they can practice breathing or counting exercises during stressful

situations.

2. **Problem-Solving:** Family members work together to identify problems in their family and devise solutions for dealing with these issues. In this exercise, they practice communication and conflict resolution skills while working through real-life problems.

3. **Talking Stick:** Talk circles allow family members to communicate with each other, promoting an accepting environment where everyone has a chance to express their thoughts and feelings without interruption. In a talking circle, a stick is passed around from one person to the next as each family member speaks and expresses themselves without interruption.

Family Values in DBT

Family values are extremely important to family DBT's success. It helps facilitate self-awareness among family members, which is the heart of this approach. Values are a set of morals guiding the decisions and actions of individuals within a unit. They allow everyone to understand acceptable behaviors within a family and give the whole unit a common purpose. Clearly defining expectations and values helps prevent conflicts and problems within the unit by creating boundaries for behavior.

Family DBT develops or identifies these common values based on what is considered healthy behaviors within the family unit.

Examples of common family values associated with DBT include:

- Honesty and open communication
- Respect for self and others
- Perseverance and resilience
- Commitment, responsibility, and reliability
- Positive self-image
- Compassion and kindness to others
- Acceptance

Strengthening these positive behaviors allows family members better communication and fosters an environment where each member feels safe, accepted, and understood. These values also help form a positive emotional atmosphere, creating a healthy support system for family members when confronted with difficult situations and tough transitions.

Ten Ways to Get the Family Involved in DBT for Your Teens

1. Schedule regular family meetings to discuss and practice DBT skills together. It allows everyone to learn and grow together, fostering unity and shared understanding.

2. Create an atmosphere where family members feel comfortable expressing their thoughts and emotions without judgment. This approach boosts honest and effective communication, leading to better problem-solving and conflict-resolution skills.

3. Be a role model for your teen by consistently practicing and demonstrating DBT skills in your life. This role modeling reinforces the importance of these skills and shows your commitment.

4. Encourage the family to work at healthy outlets for emotions, such as music, art, sports, or other activities promoting self-expression and creative thinking.

5. Eat dinner together every night, or at least have meals together as a family once a week.

6. Allow your teen to be a family leader during times of crisis. Ask for their opinions and spotlight their strengths as they help you solve the problem.

7. Find humor in life's mistakes and shortcomings. Nothing is perfect; everyone makes mistakes. Let it be an opportunity to laugh at yourselves instead of getting angry.

8. Stage a family talent show. Everyone has unique gifts and talents to share with the family, so take this time to celebrate them.

9. Give family members something to look forward to together, like a vacation or an activity everyone enjoys engaging in, especially when things are difficult at home.

10. Model problem-solving techniques in your life. Find solutions to issues and then share them with the family.

The Honesty Wheel

The honesty wheel is a great exercise to get the family together and everyone talking. It is based on the basic principle of DBT that living with acceptance, non-judgment, and respect is the foundation for healthy relationships. It helps families communicate to build trust, acceptance, and understanding. It works great anytime but is particularly useful when conflicts arise between family members.

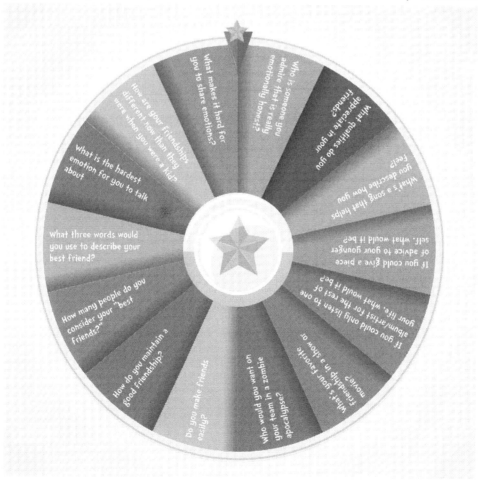

The sheet should be laid out on a flat surface, with a pen or pencil placed at the center of the wheel. Each person gets a turn to spin the pen and answer the questions it lands on. Since there are no wrong answers, the game allows parents and teens to express themselves without being judged or ridiculed. It helps families learn about each other. Overall, this game helps with conflict resolution, gratitude, and a sense of humor.

WORD SEARCH

U	V	F	H	T	D	A	T	A	I	O	R	F	L	O	W	E	R
H	L	S	J	X	C	S	Y	M	P	S	P	R	W	Q	O	I	T
Z	U	I	X	W	Q	G	F	A	L	B	F	I	Y	F	B	Y	W
R	W	K	F	B	E	V	T	P	D	A	S	E	T	C	N	L	K
S	A	T	R	E	A	S	U	R	E	H	U	N	T	E	I	O	V
N	S	D	G	A	U	U	U	I	C	K	R	D	N	G	A	R	E
A	X	V	H	S	J	N	E	L	O	O	M	S	V	P	R	G	O
E	Y	T	Z	T	T	D	T	O	R	R	A	C	S	E	R	V	U
B	A	S	K	E	T	A	A	F	A	M	I	L	Y	P	Q	E	V
Y	E	P	A	R	T	Y	L	U	T	E	P	M	B	R	V	N	E
L	C	R	T	N	U	Q	O	I	E	S	Q	N	P	E	W	P	Y
L	B	I	Y	Z	L	I	C	W	R	G	R	A	S	S	L	B	F
E	D	N	U	Y	I	P	O	I	C	G	P	W	Q	E	S	R	B
J	A	G	W	J	P	U	H	L	W	E	S	Y	D	N	A	C	E
E	Y	R	A	D	H	Q	C	E	L	E	B	R	A	T	E	Y	Q
B	I	U	E	M	W	B	I	P	Q	C	P	K	L	J	F	L	O

EASTER	CHOCOLATE	APRIL
EGGS	PRESENT	JELLYBEANS
BASKET	FAMILY	FLOWER
TREASURE HUNT	FRIENDS	GRASS
CELEBRATE	PARTY	CANDY
SPRING	CARROT	RAINBOW
DECORATE	SUNDAY	TULIP

CAMPING CHARADES

FIND AS MANY AS YOU CAN, THEN COUNT UP YOUR POINTS.
THE PERSON WITH THE MOST POINTS WINS!

MAKING A SMORE	COOKING A MEAL
SWIMMING	LOST IN THE WOODS
BEAR WALKS THROUGH CAMP	THE CANOE TIPS OVER
BUILDING A FIRE	A MOUSE IN A CAMP
YOU SEE A DEER	CATCHING FIREFLIES
READ A BOOK	SKIPPING ROCKS
USING A FLASHLIGHT	ON A HIKE
WALKING THROUGH MUD	A BEE STINGS YOU
A BUG LANDS ON YOUR HEAD	PITCHING A TENT

Total: ⬭

Total: ⬭

Total: ⬭

Total: ⬭

A-Z RACE

DON'T START UNTIL WE SAY GO!

Write EASTER-related words that starts with each
letter from A-Z. The first one with the most unique
answers is the winner!

A _____

B _____

C _____

D _____

E _____

F _____

G _____

H _____

I _____

J _____

K _____

L _____

M _____

N _____

O _____

P _____

Q _____

R _____

S _____

T _____

U _____

V _____

W _____

X _____

Y _____

Z _____

SCAVENGER HUNT

SCAVENGER HUNT

- ◯ BUNNY
- ◯ CARROT
- ◯ JELLY BEANS
- ◯ YELLOW EASTER EGG
- ◯ CROSS
- ◯ SOMETHING BLUE

- ◯ CHOCOLATE BUNNY
- ◯ FLOWERS
- ◯ BIRD
- ◯ CANDY
- ◯ EASTER BASKET
- ◯ PINK EASTER EGG

WORD SCRAMBLE

YOU HAVE 3 MINUTES TO UNSCRAMBLE THE WORDS BELOW. THE PERSON WHO UNSCRAMBLES THE MOST WORDS CORRECTLY WINS!

1. ETNT
2. ERFI
3. ECMAPTIS
4. OHACMKM
5. ESETR
6. PAKSANC
7. IGAPMNC
8. SURIESN
9. REAB
10. ASANIML
11. ESOSIRT
12. RAMLLSAMHSOW
13. ANIOMUTN
14. AERUTN
15. OSODOUTR

BINGO

FIND-THE-GUEST BINGO

Find someone who matches the bingo squares.
Get them to write their name in the square.
First one to get BINGO wins!

Decorated Easter eggs this year	Favorite color is pink	Loves marshmallow peeps	Is vegan or vegetarian	Was borned in April
Is wearing something with polka dots	Can play a musical instrument	Loud	Has Easter eggs	Went on vacation recently
Loves Hip Hop Music	Participated in an egg hunt		Baked Easter treats this year	Is an only child
Got up before 7am today	Loves jelly beans	Is on spring break	Is wearing pastels	Loves hot cross buns
Ate chocolate today	Is wearing bunny ears	Went to church today	Loves to garden	Can roll their tongue

TRIVIA

Test your EASTER knowledge. Most correct answers wins!

1. What color were the first Easter eggs dyed?
   A. Blue   B. Yellow   C. Red

2. What flower is considered an Easter symbol?
   A. Lily   B. Tulip   C. Daisy

3. Easter is commemorated as the day that Jesus was:
   A. Born   B. Resurrected   C. Baptized

4. Where is the largest Easter egg museum in the world?
   A. Germany   B. Ukraine   C. Sweden

5. What country did the Easter Bunny tradition originate?
   A. Germany   B. Poland   C. France

6. What do white Easter Lilies represent?
   A. Optimism   B. wisdom   C. Purity

7. What is the date of Easter determined by?
   A. Weather   B. The moon   C. Date of the month

8. What egg-shaped candy is illegal in the United States?
   A. Cadbury   B. Kinder surprise   C. Robin eggs

9. What kind of meat is often associated with Easter?
   A. Lamb   B. Turkey   C. Pork

10. The most popular American Easter candy is:
    A. Peeps   B. Jelly Beans   C. Cadbury egg

WORD SEARCH

```
N O Q I M S N K N F Z F A P D H Z I T L
S L E G N A I D Z L F D E K W L Z U C G
H D I H W Y C D X N V R J T A Z L V B B
R C E X X G E X F D M B U G I Z H U Y R
X J D J K M M S R E I C G G B H Q Y B N
H G W L R C F F F I H V A N Q L W K X O
C G P R K O T A F U L Z J R I P Y F R I
C S U W N N I K W O J M E W G N M B M N
X K T Y N O U E P V P A D F A U A Z W U
P U I O L M P S G R G R U I I W G E B E
L Y W N C E Y O X S I U T A M H E T M R
L D Z F V K V R J J V O I L J C Y A K Y
U E E B S I I I R T I H T B T Z T R A L
D C N P X N T N L H N S A C R W L Y M I
Q O L D Z W C I G O G O R Y S H B A R M
J R Q Q J D B F N F J T G L O J X K O A
M A Z Z N S W L V G M A P M F B K R H F
Y T A Y M T L I F B V V N T D Q D Q Y X
O E V L O C Y K T T R E E H K R Q W D R
Q D D Y H L E P S O G P L K K B M O F M
```

ANGELS   DECORATED
FAMILY REUNION   GIVING
GOSPEL   GRATITUDE
INVITING   LIVELY
MEANING   MYRRH
NICE   STOCKING
TREE   WHITE

Chapter 10: Moving Forward: Empowering Your Teenager

Some of the greatest shifts in your teenager's life will occur during this age. They are on the cusp of entering adulthood but are still young and have plenty of time to observe, analyze, and learn from the world. Your duty is to guide them through these changes and teach them about what is to come.

Like any other time in their life, they need support, guidance, and help from you to navigate the challenges and opportunities that lie ahead. However, empowering your teenager and encouraging them to take ownership of their decisions and actions is also important. It will foster their independence and self-confidence and equip them with the necessary skills to face the world beyond their teenage years. Empowering your teenager involves striking a delicate balance between providing guidance and allowing them the freedom to make their own choices while supporting them through their successes and failures.

Empowering your teens will lead them to become more independent.
https://pixabay.com/vectors/female-woman-women-girl-power-3285623/

It can be tempting to want to control every aspect of your teenager's life in an effort to protect them, but the truth is that part of their growth and development is learning from their experiences and mistakes. Empowering them to make decisions teaches them valuable life skills like problem-solving, critical thinking, and responsibility. Through these experiences, they develop self-reliance and confidence.

Here are some of the many ways you can nurture their independence as you guide your teenager through this transition:

1. Offer Reassurance

Even though your teenager is about to take on the world as a young adult, they will still need reassurance that you are there for them. They might have questions about how their life and the world will be beyond the safety of the nest. Reassuring them that you will support and guide them through this transition helps dissipate some of their anxiety. Moreover, they will more likely reach out to you when they need help or want your input on an important decision.

2. Encourage Risk-Taking

You can't make the journey from childhood to adulthood without taking some risks. Your teen will undoubtedly take risks that don't turn out quite as well as they hoped, but if you don't allow them this freedom, they won't learn valuable life lessons.

3. Emphasize Independence

You might be tempted to do everything for your teenager, especially during a rough patch. However, empowering them allows them the space and opportunity to work through their issues independently. If you are always swooping in to save the day, they won't develop the life skills to handle difficult situations.

4. Highlight the Importance of Short-Term and Long-Term Goals

You should help your teenager identify short-term and long-term goals. They can be anything from an end-of-year school project to getting a college scholarship. Having a long-term goal to strive for gives your teenager something to focus their energy on and will motivate them to work toward some of their short-term goals. It is another way to encourage them to take some risks and make the most of their experiences.

5. Acknowledge Their Achievements

Acknowledging your teenager's achievements reinforces that their hard work and efforts are worth something. No one wants to work hard on something only to receive indifference, so rewarding their hard work with praise and meaningful gifts helps them understand their efforts are important and appreciated. It doesn't matter if they don't quite reach the goal as they had hoped; recognizing them for the effort is enough.

S. M. A. R. T Goal Sheet

S.M.A.R.T. goal setting (specific, measurable, action, realistic, and timely) is a great way to ensure your teenager's goals are attainable and rewarding. It is a structured and highly strategic system that helps your teenager set achievable and measurable goals as you guide them through this important phase in their life. Use this worksheet or questionnaire to guide your teen through the S.M.A.R.T. goal steps.

MAKE YOUR GOALS

Setting goals can be a great way to challenge yourself to make healthy lifestyle changes. Set yourself up for success by making your goals SMART!

SPECIFIC	MEASURABLE	ATTAINABLE	RELEVANT	TIMELY
What is your goal?	How will you keep track of your progress?	How will you achieve your goal? Make a plan!	How will this goal help you?	When will you achieve this goal?

 MY GOAL IS: _____

e.g. To drink more water! I will aim for 6 cups per day

 I WILL TRACK MY PROGRESS BY: _____

_____

e.g. I will track my progress by logging how many glasses I drink each day in my phone or planner

 I WILL ACHIEVE THIS GOAL BY DOING THE FOLLOWING: _____

_____

e.g. 1. Keep a clear bottle with me so I can tell how much I've had   2. Set an alarm to remind myself to drink every 2 hours

 THIS GOAL HELPS ME BECAUSE: _____

_____

e.g. This goal will help me to be healthier, have more energy, and help my skin

 I WILL COMPLETE THIS GOAL BY (DATE): _____

_____

e.g. I will achieve my goal by February 15th

You can print as many sheets as you like. By answering these questions, your teen will get an idea of what they want from life and what is realistically possible to achieve. They will develop ownership over their goals and feel more empowered as they pursue these new experiences, and you will be right there to offer a gentle nudge in the right direction if needed.

Bonus Section: 20 Top DBT Tips for Parents

1. If you feel irritable over your teenager, keep a picture of them nearby as a toddler. It's the same creature, only with different abilities and changed needs.

2. It is a gift when your teenager makes mistakes. You can teach them an important lesson about their behavior when they do.

3. It is okay if your teenager argues with you. See it as an opportunity to practice your listening skills.

4. Don't push back when your teen says they need space because it allows them to go through their thoughts from their end. Instead, ask how you can support their decision.

5. Don't always assume your teenager is defying you. Practice the wisdom of assuming the best in your teen in their honesty, integrity, and effort.

6. Do your best not to focus on what isn't working in your teenager's life (or yours). Acknowledge what is working, too.

7. Don't try so hard to fix a problem that you create a bigger one.

8. Don't forget your teenager is growing physically, emotionally, and mentally. It is okay if the changes evoke anxiety; embrace the change enthusiastically because it is growth.

9. Give your teenager a voice and ask for their input in making rules and family plans.

10. Don't become isolated from your teenager because of conflicting ideas. Accept that they might have a different view of the world than you.

11. Ask your teenager questions to help them reflect on their behavior. "What do you think caused this?" "What is your plan now?" "How can I support this?"

12. Don't always assume your teen is like every other teen in their behavior and personality.

13. Active listening is a powerful skill to use with your teenager. Focus on what they say rather than how it makes you feel.

14. Don't give up when trying to connect with your teenager. It is a marathon, not a sprint.

15. Don't take your anger and resentment about your parents out on your teenager. They are not them. Treat your teenager with the same courtesy, acceptance, and forgiveness you would like to receive.

16. Don't over-parent by interfering too much in their life. Sometimes, they know what they need without you having to tell them.

17. Lecturing hardly works; rather, listen and ask questions.

18. Don't take their anger personally. Instead, see it as a call for help. Take a moment to acknowledge their feelings, then ask what they need from you.

19. Don't feel guilty for not knowing everything about your teenager. No parent does.

20. Don't lose your sense of humor.

Conclusion

Parenting is a challenging journey, especially when faced with the unique struggles that come with raising a teenager. In addition to dealing with discipline, teaching them about independence, and developing their own identity, you also have to contend with the pressures of high school. As a parent, there's a lot on your plate when it comes to teaching your child and helping them discover who they really are. To make life easier for both of you, focus on the things that matter, like accepting and embracing their emotions, the importance of teamwork, and the effects of their choices. Having a realistic view of your child's behavior and working with them instead of against them is important. With just a little bit of TLC, you can work through any problems that arise and bring out the best in both of you.

As you embark on this transformative journey, know that you are not alone; a vast network of helpful resources is available to parents like you worldwide. From parenting books and online forums to therapy and support groups, you can find guidance and support from professionals and parents who have walked a similar path. These resources provide valuable insight, practical strategies, and a sense of community, making the journey through adolescence less daunting. It's okay to ask for help and lean on others during this phase. Building a strong support system benefits your child and gives you the emotional stability and inner strength to raise a competent, well-adjusted, and confident teenager. So don't shoulder the burden alone. Remember, raising a teenager is hard work, and there is no easy answer. However, with a little patience and persistence, you'll have a phenomenal teen on your hands!

Quick Notes

What did you learn from the book? Write it all down and take it everywhere you go!

Check out another book in the series

References

Bernstein, J. (2018, January 2). Mindfulness for Teen Worry: Quick and Easy Strategies to Let Go of Anxiety, Worry, and Stress.

Dijk, S. V. (2016, January 1). Surviving the Emotional Roller Coaster: DBT Skills to Help Teens Manage Emotions.

Dijk, S. V., & Guindon, K. (2010, March 1). The Bipolar Workbook for Teens: DBT Skills to Help You Control Mood Swings.

Forte, J. (2023, April 4). Coping Skills & Emotional Regulation for Teens: Conquer Anxiety, Master Your Emotions & Build Unstoppable Self-Confidence.

Glasser, J. M. (2013, November 30). Learning to Feel Good and Stay Cool: Emotional Regulation Tools for Kids with Ad/HD.

Harvey, P., & Rathbone, B. H. (2015, December 1). Parenting a Teen Who Has Intense Emotions: DBT Skills to Help Your Teen Navigate Emotional and Behavioral Challenges.

McKay, M., Wood, J. C., & Brantley, J. (2019, October 1). The Dialectical Behavior Therapy Skills Workbook: Practical DBT Exercises for Learning Mindfulness, Interpersonal Effectiveness, Emotion Regulation, and Distress Tolerance.

McKay, M., Wood, J. C., & Brantley, J. (2020, November 1). Pocket Therapy for Emotional Balance: Quick DBT Skills to Manage Intense Emotions.

Purcell, M. C., & Murphy, J. R. (2014, April 1). Mindfulness for Teen Anger: A Workbook to Overcome Anger and Aggression Using MBSR and DBT Skills.

Rathus, J. H., & Miller, A. L. (2014, November 20). DBT Skills Manual for Adolescents. Guilford Press, The.

Made in the USA
Columbia, SC
27 November 2024

47701117R00046